Systematic Reuse:
Issues in Initiating and Improving a Reuse Program

Springer
London
Berlin
Heidelberg
New York
Barcelona
Budapest
Hong Kong
Milan
Paris
Santa Clara
Singapore
Tokyo

Marjan Sarshar (Ed.)

Systematic Reuse:

Issues in Initiating and Improving a Reuse Program

Proceedings of the International Workshop on Systematic Reuse, Liverpool, 8-9 January 1996

BCS Software Reuse Specialist Group Series

Springer

Marjan Sarshar, BSc (Hons), MSc, PhD, CEng, MIEE

School of Computing and Mathematical Sciences
Liverpool John Moores University, Byrom Street,
Liverpool, L3 3AF, UK

ISBN-13:978-3-540-76012-2 e-ISBN-13:978-1-4471-1484-0
DOI: 10.1007/978-1-4471-1484-0

British Library Cataloguing in Publication Data
A Catalogue record for this book is available from the British Library

Typesetting: Camera ready by editor

34/3830-543210 Printed on acid-free paper

Preface

This book contains the papers presented at the International Workshop on Systematic Reuse, held in Liverpool (UK) in January 1996. The Workshop was aimed at industrialists and researchers who are involved in reuse programmes. The book provides practical advice from those who had been involved in reuse introduction in a large number of industrial sectors.

Compared to other engineering disciplines, software engineering is still a craft. Reuse is the technology which promises to transform the industry from craft to engineering production. However, experiences with systematic reuse in the past years prove that reuse introduces many people, process and technical issues. It is important to keep focused on cultural and management issues. Investment in reuse pays off over a long period. Management must set realistic expectations and be prepared to manage multidimensional change.

It is often claimed that there are no off the shelf solutions for implementing reuse. However, reuse is becoming of age. Many companies are reporting successful reuse programmes. A few examples are IBM, Hitachi, Hewlett-Packard, AT&T. This book presents some of the common trends in terms of the experiences and problems that are emerging.

Each chapter within the book focuses on a significant implementation issue. The chapters do not present ready made solutions. They familiarise the reader with the topic and provide pragmatic guidance. We hope that this can generate further discussions among the reuse community and pave the way for widespread reuse adoption.

Marjan Sarshar
Liverpool John Moores University

Ben Whittle
BCS Reuse Special Interest Group chairperson

Contents

Contributors

Roger Chambers
National Westminster Bank
Information Management, IT Delivery
Level A/3 West
74 Alie Street
London E1 8HL, UK

Charles Church, BSc (Hons), PhD
Advanced Software Centre
Hitachi Europe Ltd
Maidenhead, UK

Dario de Judicibus, PhD
IBM Rome Networking Software Laboratory
Piazzale Giulio Pastore 6
I-00 1 44 Roma, Italy

Jack Hassal
Stanford Software Ltd
The Hollygate, Chestergate
Stockport, Cheshire SK3 0BD, UK

Eric Leach, BSc
ELM Ltd
2 Bell Road, Hounslow
Middlesex TW3 3NN, UK

Jean-Marc Morel
BULL S.A.
Rue Jean JAURES - F-78340
Les Clayes-sous-bois
France

Ruben Prieto-Díaz, B.S., M.S., PhD
Reuse, Inc.
12365, Washington Brice Road
Fairfax, VA22033, USA

Suzanne Robertson
The Atlantic Systems Guild Ltd
11 St Mary's Terrace
London W2 1SU, UK

Ben Whittle, B.A., MSc, PhD
Rolls-Royce UTC
University of York
York YO1 5DD, UK

Reuse as a New Paradigm for Software Development

Rubén Prieto-Díaz
Reuse, Inc.
Fairfax, VA U.S.A.

Abstract

This paper discusses why software is hard to reuse and why we can not extend reuse analogies in other fields to software. It explores tensions in reuse caused by granularity and abstraction level and argues for a different way of developing software. The proposed new approach is reuse based and results in systematic reuse. The paper explores what is necessary for accomplishing systematic reuse and recommends the use of a domain analysis tool, DARE, to get started.

KEYWORDS: systematic reuse, domain analysis, software development.

1 Introduction

The concept of reuse in engineering is simple. It has been successfully applied in several areas, from civil engineering to electronics. In fact most engineering disciplines are based on the reuse concept from components to formulas to ideas. Despite several years of trying to bring reuse to practice, software engineers have found out that reuse in software is not the same as in other areas, that software is very hard to reuse.

In the following sections we discuss why software is hard to reuse and compare ad-hoc and systematic reuse. We propose a model for enabling systematic reuse and provide some recommendations for starting.

Section 2 compares engineering practices in traditional engineering with software engineering practices; Section 3 analyzes tensions in reuse caused by granularity and abstraction level, and how to overcome them; Section 4 compares ad-hoc and systematic reuse; Section 5 proposes a reuse based software development model that results in systematic reuse; and Section 6 recommends a tool, DARE, for starting the process.

2 Reuse as an Implicit Practice

There are not reuse sub disciplines in traditional engineering fields. Electrical engineers, for example, do not take explicit reuse courses nor are there conferences or symposia on circuits reuse issues. Reuse is an implicit practice in traditional engineering fields. We compare in this section the traditional engineering practice with software engineering practice. Contrary to belief, they are different, and that difference is part of the reason why reuse is not widely practiced in the software industry.

2.1 Reuse in Traditional Engineering

Reuse in traditional engineering is part of the engineering process. In aeronautical design, for example, engineers had thought that airfoils exhibit certain performance characteristics based on their geometry and that lift to drag ratio is an important factor of an airfoil. When designing a wing, an airfoil is usually selected from a catalog of tested and certified airfoils (e.g., NACA). An airfoil defines the cross section geometry of a wing and defines most of the wing characteristics. The selection is based on the wing performance requirements.

Aeronautical engineers are trained to make the best possible choice of airfoils by considering the requirements and selecting an airfoil that provides the best balance of parameters—a good design vs. the best design. In most cases, an airfoil satisfies some but not all the requirements.

What goes on in this selection process is a continuous adjustment and evaluation of the requirements. That is, if the mission requirements call for a very low stall speed and a low drag coefficient, and there is one airfoil that satisfies better the former and another that satisfies better the latter, then the mission requirements are typically modified to accommodate the performance provided by the selected airfoil. If the requirements can not be compromised, the only alternative is to create an airfoil that satisfies all of them. Such approach would require great expense in going through the whole analysis and certification process.

The next question would be: is the requirement worth the expense? In most practical situations it is not. One reason is that the reusable objects in this example—airfoil specifications, are difficult and expensive to create. This fact is even more prominent in the hardware world (e.g., integrated circuits in electronics design.)

Practice in making the choice that provides the best balance in the requirements and the one that does not compromise key requirements is what makes a good engineer. Engineers are, therefore, good reusers by training, even if they never took a reuse course. Their job is, in fact, to reuse.

2.2 Reuse in Software Engineering

The state of the practice in software engineering has been, by far, to blindly satisfy the given requirements. Significant work has been done on requirements verification, that is, to ascertain that a final design or product truly satisfies the given requirements. This implies that once a set of requirements are given, and accepted, they are never questioned. The goal of the software engineer is to satisfy them, completely and correctly.

A software engineer, therefore, is more of a programmer than an engineer. Design trade-offs in relation to requirements and what can be delivered is typically done at requirements analysis and specification time. This does not mean that the software engineer is totally excluded from trade-off analyses, but, that his scope is restricted mainly to performance issues.

Unfortunately, software engineers are not trained like other conventional engineers—to make optimum trade-off decisions. Implicit reuse is not part of their regular practice, reuse is explicit and has to be acquired later. In fact, except for modern software engineering courses, software engineering students have been typically trained for individual work where they are asked to create their own programs from scratch. This would be tantamount to ask aeronautical engineering students to create airfoils in order to be able to design wings, or electronics engineering students to create integrated chips in order to design computers.

This situation is but a logical result of the nature of software. By being "soft" it implies that, like plaster, it can be molded to fit any shape. Trade-offs belong to the domain of "hard" objects, those that can not be changed, at least not easily. Why bother with trade-offs if we can always fit our software to any requirement?

2.3 Making Software Hard

It seems that software's main advantage—its softness—is suddenly becoming its major liability. As long as we see software as a malleable object, agreeing on conventions and standards will be a continuous uphill battle. How can we inject some element of hardness into software to make it more amenable to standardization? One answer is complexity. By making software elements more complex it becomes less attractive to create them and more attractive to reuse them.

Defining sets of standard domain specific software components could be a relatively straight forward process. Committees of domain experts could analyze their own domains, identify common functions, engineer them, and declare them the standard components. This idealized standardization is in sharp contrast with reality. In the world of software it is the market who defines the standards, and those standards are not necessary the best (e.g., DOS, Windows.) Standards evolve, for the most part, not by imposing them (e.g., Ada) but by free choice (e.g., C, Unix.)

Visual Basic and its exploding industry of VB ad-ons is a clear example of both arguments: complexity stimulates reuse, and market trends define standards.

Making software components harder to create and easier to buy will stimulate software engineers to become true designers in the traditional engineering sense—to practice genuine trade-off analysis.

Applications involving Visual Basic, for example, will call for use of commercially available components. Such applications will exhibit, with time, certain common features that will be adopted as standards.

The role of the software engineer will resemble more closely the role of a traditional engineer: selecting the best combination of existing components that will generate a "good," not necessarily the "best," design. And one that will force some compromises on the requirements.

3 Tensions in Reuse

There are two software factors that generate tension in software reuse: granularity and abstraction level. Granularity is the size of the component to be reused. Small components are fine granules and large components are coarse granules. Abstraction levels range from code at the lowest level to requirements definitions at the highest.

Both, granularity and abstraction are at opposite ends of trade-offs in reuse pay-off and ease of reuse.

3.1 Granularity

Reuse pay-off is proportional to component size. The larger the component we can reuse, the higher the pay-off. The savings will be higher for reusing a 100 KLOC component than by reusing a 1 KLOC component. However, reusing the 1 KLOC component may be easier than reusing the 100 KLOC one. It may be very likely that the large component can be used only as a "white box" while a small component has a higher probability of being encapsulated as a "black box."

These tensions are shown in Figure 1. Since both goals are contradictory, there is a need of a careful trade-off analysis to achieve an acceptable component size that will reasonably satisfy both goals most of the time. Focusing on one goal, say, high pay-off, can generate large components that are so difficult to reuse that the cost of reusing them offsets the potential pay-off gains.

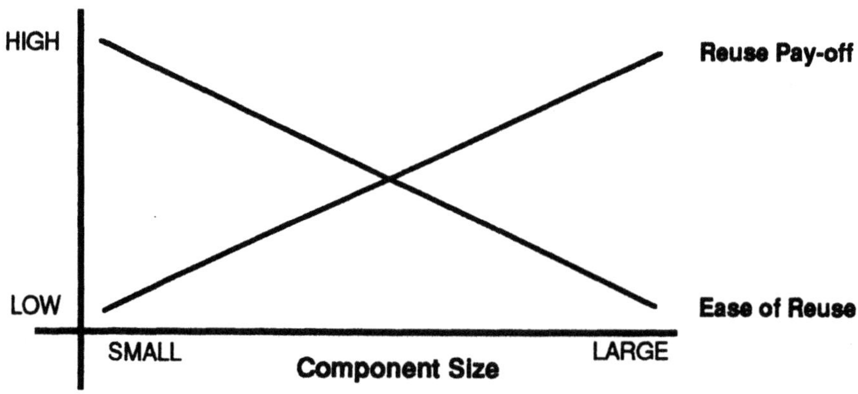

Figure 1 Reuse Tension Caused by Component Size

3.2 Abstraction Level

The abstraction level of reusable components generates a similar tension between reuse pay-off and ease of reuse. Reuse at the requirements level generates a higher pay-off than reusing at the code level. By the time we reach the code level in the software life cycle and we are ready to look for a reusable component, we have spent already over 40% of the life cycle cost. If we are able, instead, to identify reusable requirements right at the start of our software development process, the reuse pay-off will be significantly higher.

An important assumption in this argument is that reusable requirements propagate reuse to the code level. That is, when we reuse a set of requirements, we are also reusing all their products down stream in the life cycle.

Reusable requirements are typically white box components. Since they are expressed at a high level of abstraction, we need to fill several implementation details as we progress down into design and coding. Reuse is therefore more difficult. Code components, on the other hand, can be made into black boxes (i.e., object classes) and reused easily. Figure 2 shows reuse tension caused by abstraction level. Figures 1 and 2 are basically identical except for the labeling in their abscissas.

In dealing with abstraction levels we face a similar difficulty with trade-offs as we face dealing with component size. We need to find the combination that generates the best reuse most of the times.

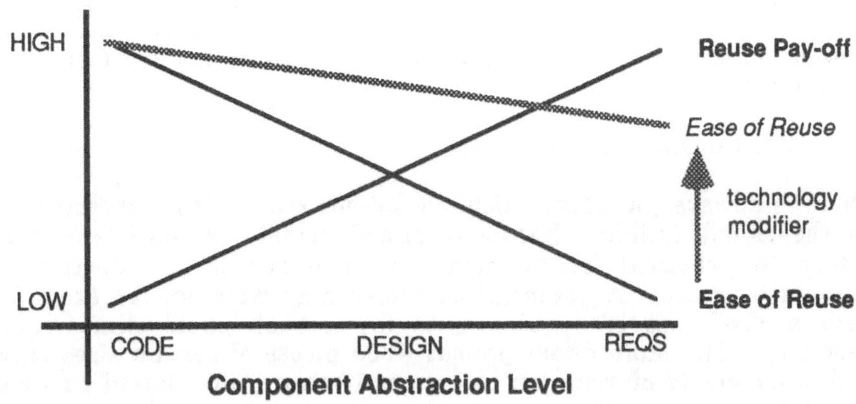

Figure 2 Reuse Tension Caused by Component Abstraction Level

3.3 Improving Reuse

The reuse pay-off curves in both cases can not be changed. Reuse pay-off is independent of technology—it is a fact. The ease of reuse curve, however, can be altered with methods and technology. What we want is to advance reuse technology to make reuse easy for all component sizes and for all levels of abstraction. This desirable state (shown in Figure 2 as a shaded ease of reuse curve modified by technology) does not come free. Significant amount of analysis and planning is required as well as some key tools that support the process.

4 Ad-hoc vs. Systematic Reuse

In this section we compare and contrast ad-hoc and systematic reuse. We argue that systematic reuse is the only way to improve reuse and propose a new model for software development based on systematic reuse.

4.1 Ad-hoc Reuse

The view that reuse libraries are all that is needed for a successful reuse practice is no longer true. The perception that effective reuse libraries can be created by collecting existing software is also a fallacy. Both ideas are the result of what we call ad-hoc or opportunistic reuse. Ad-hoc reuse is based on the idea that, as a software system is developed, we can stop at selected life cycle stages, consult the reuse library, and find something we can reuse. That the reuse library is populated with an assortment of components collected from several applications [1].

Although useful, ad-hoc reuse offers limited pay-off. Ad-hoc reuse is informal and conducted at the individual level. It is difficult also to find matches for requirements in libraries of general components. Components in these libraries are so specific and narrow that their adaptation to a new set of requirements is usually too expensive and counterproductive.

4.1.1 The Hardware Store Model

There is however, a market niche for ad-hoc reuse. It is characterized by the "home builders hardware store" model. A hardware store caters to practical handy men. It provides large selection of "standard" parts. A potential customer may walk in, for example, with a draft set of requirements for a book shelf—dimensions, geometry. The store offers pre-cut wood pieces of certain sizes only, and assortments of standard nails, wood screws, etc. Based on what is available, the customer needs to re-consider its requirements and re-design the book shelf using the available hardware store components.

The customer in this case is definitely a craftsman, and most likely, an amateur craftsman. A professional book shelf carpenter would not go to a hardware store, he would have his own shop and buy raw wood. The success of the hardware store model is its large inventory and variability, and the existence of a large market of do-it-yourself individuals. Although a successful model, it does not scale up to industrial production.

4.1.2 *Ad-hoc Reuse Limits*

Experience with several general libraries and with opportunistic reuse programs has demonstrated that factors above 50% reuse are difficult to achieve with ad-hoc reuse alone [2].

Unfortunately, the mainstream of research and development in software reusability has focused on improving ad-hoc reuse. This trend lasted for several years. It was during this time that new approaches were proposed for library classification, retrieval, cataloging, and reusable component designs. The results were positive but reuse figures did not improve.

4.2 Systematic Reuse

It has been only recently that systematic reuse has entered the mainstream in the reuse community [3]. Systematic reuse, however, has been proposed and practiced in industry since the early 80's [4, 5, 6].

It was realized during the height of ad-hoc reuse research, that library components have to be designed and created to be reusable. That they need to fit into a specific place in a predefined architecture. Otherwise, reuse would improve software productivity only marginally.

Systematic reuse is when reuse has been planned in an organization. When its practice has been formalized, guidelines and procedures have been established, and a generic, common architecture has been defined. This common architecture captures the essential features and possible variabilities of the applications to be developed. Another characteristic of systematic reuse is that an assessment and evaluation based on reuse metrics need to be established for continuous improvement.

4.2.1 *The Assembly Line Model*

Establishing a systematic reuse program is significantly more expensive than practicing ad-hoc reuse. In contrast with the hardware store model for ad-hoc reuse, systematic reuse can be illustrated with the "assembly line" model in a manufacturing plant.

An assembly line consists of an infrastructure of special machines and processes that enable mass production of a specific class of products. An assembly line requires substantial investment. The production process must be carefully analyzed, the assembly components designed for smooth fitting, and special tooling created. Simulation of the assembly line is also needed as well as procedures for measuring its performance.

An assembly line is a natural evolution from single, craftsmanship style production. In order to design an assembly line, we need substantial knowledge and experience on how to craft single items—we need to be domain experts. Evolution of the auto industry at the turn of the century is a good example.

Another observation is that within a reasonable range, an assembly line can be tailored to support some variations of a product. A bottling plant, for example, can be adjusted to support different bottle sizes or different drink mixtures, or an auto plant to support different car options. On the other hand, trying to modify an assembly plant designed for TV sets to produce photographic cameras would be unthinkable. The former is the equivalent of domain variabilities, the latter, to trying to reuse across domains.

A fact, however, is that once an assembly line goes into production, production cost per item produced is orders of magnitude cheaper than individually crafting them.

4.2.2 Implications of Systematic Reuse

These analogies help us understand better the advantages, limitations, and difficulties in implementing systematic reuse. We need to create an infrastructure, analyze the domain, derive domain models (of the products we want to produce,) define processes, and establish performance measures for continuous improvement.

In contrast with industrial engineering, where the design and creation of manufacturing plants has reached maturity, software engineers are just beginning to understand its implications. One recurring implication is that software is "soft" and difficult to define, not tangible like typical products in an assembly line.

Another implication is that, contrary to a manufacturing plant where products of a fixed design are mass produced, in systematic reuse, we have to produce multitude of designs, one for each product whose production run is usually one.

A third implication is that it would be difficult to modify a reuse infrastructure for a specific domain to be used in a different domain. A software example is trying to modify a COBOL compiler to compile C code. Fortunately, compiler construction is a mature domain and we can find tools for generating compilers.

A fourth implication of systematic reuse is that there are not models or techniques yet for predicting or estimating reuse performance of a reuse infrastructure. We can not predict accurately the economic benefit of a systematic reuse program. We can only infer from similar experiences.

In summary, systematic reuse offers a high pay-off but it is not free. In fact it is very expensive to establish a reuse infrastructure for systematic reuse.

5 Reuse Based Software Development

Systematic reuse requires a paradigm shift in the software development process—a move from craftsmanship to mass production. The conventional waterfall model of software development is the prime example of craftsmanship production—creation of single software applications. Systematic reuse requires a new model for software development, one based on reuse.

In this section we look at a model for a reuse infrastructure based on domain analysis and explore issues of its applicability.

5.1 A Model for a Reuse Infrastructure

A reuse based software development model follows the assembly line analogy. It is built around a reuse infrastructure. Figure 3 shows a model for reuse based software development. The infrastructure is depicted by the boxes surrounding the software development box. A key element of the infrastructure is domain analysis.

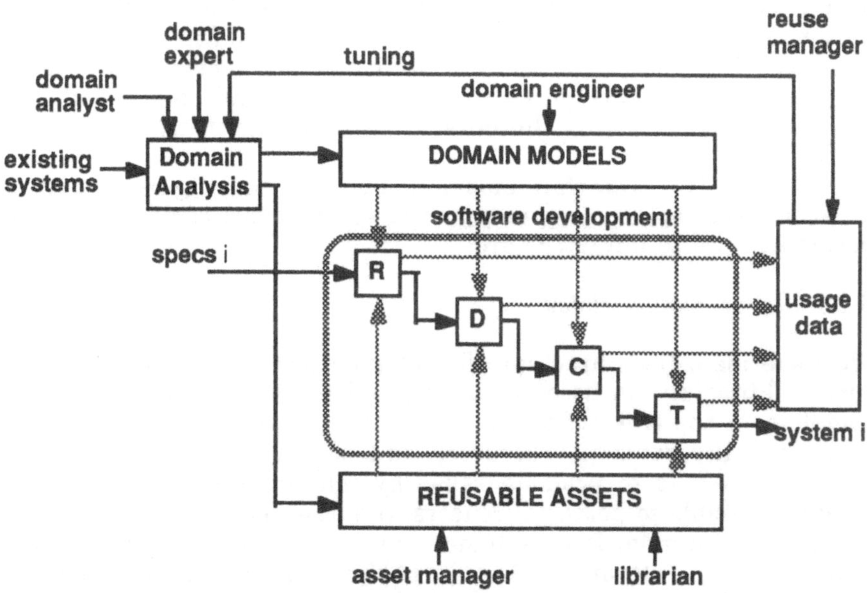

Figure 3 A Reuse Infrastructure

5.1.1 Domain Analysis

During domain analysis information is collected from existing systems in the form of source code, documentation, designs, user manuals, and test plans, together with domain knowledge and requirements for current and future systems. A domain analyst together with one or more domain experts extract relevant information and knowledge. They analyze and abstract it. With the support of a domain engineer, knowledge and abstractions are organized and encapsulated in the form of domain models, standards, and collections of reusable components. The process is guided by domain analysis methods and techniques as well as management procedures.

Domain models, reusable assets, and a reuse performance evaluation process (usage data box) constitute the rest of the infrastructure. Domain models, in a variety of forms, support (i.e., control) the different phases of software development.

5.1.2 Using the Infrastructure

We have chosen the waterfall model in Figure 3 to illustrate how the infrastructure supports each of the waterfall stages: requirements (R), design (D), coding (C), and testing (C). A typical project would start with a set of needs (specs) and terminate with a working system. For each stage in the process, the infrastructure is used to provide models and reusable components, and at each stage, reuse performance is evaluated for improving the infrastructure.

For example, at the design phase (D), design models for the class of systems being designed are searched from the domain models library. After evaluation one is selected. Instantiations of the selected design available from the reusable assets library are evaluated and selected. Information on the reusability of the models and assets is reported back (via usage data) to domain analysis for refining the models and for updating the library. This results in an improvement of the infrastructure.

Although the waterfall model is used in this figure, other approaches like rapid prototyping or the spiral model could also be supported by a reuse infrastructure.

5.1.3 Infrastructure Roles

We have identified three specific roles critical to a reuse infrastructure: a librarian, an asset manager, and a reuse manager. All three complement the tasks of the domain analyst, experts, and engineer by managing the reusable resources and collecting information. The librarian task is to promote reuse by making assets available and easily accessible to potential reusers, the asset manager controls asset quality and standards compliance, and the reuse manager supports data collection relevant to domain analysis and coordinates the overall reuse effort.

A reuse library system is necessary to support all the tasks and processes of a reuse infrastructure.

5.2 The Reuse Based Paradigm

The model for a reuse infrastructure presented calls for some radical changes in the practice of software development. One of these changes is that instead of one life cycle, we need now to pay attention to two life cycles: one for the products and one for the refinement of the infrastructure. Both life cycles are dependent.

The infrastructure life cycle is a continuous process that transcends individual applications. One challenge is to keep the participation of the infrastructure life cycle for a large number of system developments.

In contrast with creating a typical assembly plant, creating a reuse infrastructure is more of a learning process. Physical objects like bottles and cars, we can define accurately and completely before mass producing them. Software systems we can't. We can provide an initial set of requirements, but, they will change as we develop the system. A reuse infrastructure, therefore, must be created over time as we develop several applications in the same domain. An initial bootstrap infrastructure is necessary to start the process. This initial infrastructure can be produced with domain analysis.

6 DARE

DARE (Domain Analysis and Reuse Environment) is a tool that supports the domain analysis process and can be used for starting a bootstrap reuse infrastructure. DARE focus is in the initial discovery and structuring of domain models. Its users see their domain analysis job as one of producing a domain analysis book that contains all domain analysis inputs, domain analysis outputs, and supporting material for using the book (table of contents, indices, etc.) and for understanding the book (glossary citations, analysis parameters, etc.) A VisualBasic DARE prototype is currently being developed jointly by Reuse, Inc. and the Software Engineering Guild, Fairfax, VA. [7]

6.1 DARE Process Model

Figure 4 is a graphical summary of DARE's process model. There are three major components to the domain analysis process: document analysis, code analysis, and analysis of domain expert information.

The initial processing of document sources are scanning—automatically inputting documents with a scanner, and lexical analysis—breaking the text into words. Three types of operation then take place: filtering (including stoplist creation and stemming), the calculation of lexical affinities, and the creation of indexes. Document source information is used in term clustering, or the organizing of terms into semantic clusters. Some term clustering is done automatically and some manually. Term clustering is the first phase in faceted classification of the vocabulary in the domain.

Expert information is derived via manual knowledge acquisition. This information is captured using knowledge representation methods. Information from code sources is derived with code static analysis tools. The resulting program structure information is used to perform commonality analyses—the identification of common parts and structures of the various systems in the domain.

All domain information resides in the domain book. A window based user interface provides navigational support and invokes the tools necessary for the several processes.

Users interact with the database via a windowed interface to extract and analyze data about domains. DARE provides tools to set up and administer such databases.

DARE is supported by a detailed domain analysis method. The DARE DA method is an extended and customized version of the Domain Analysis Process Model developed as part of the STARS Reuse Library Process Model [8].

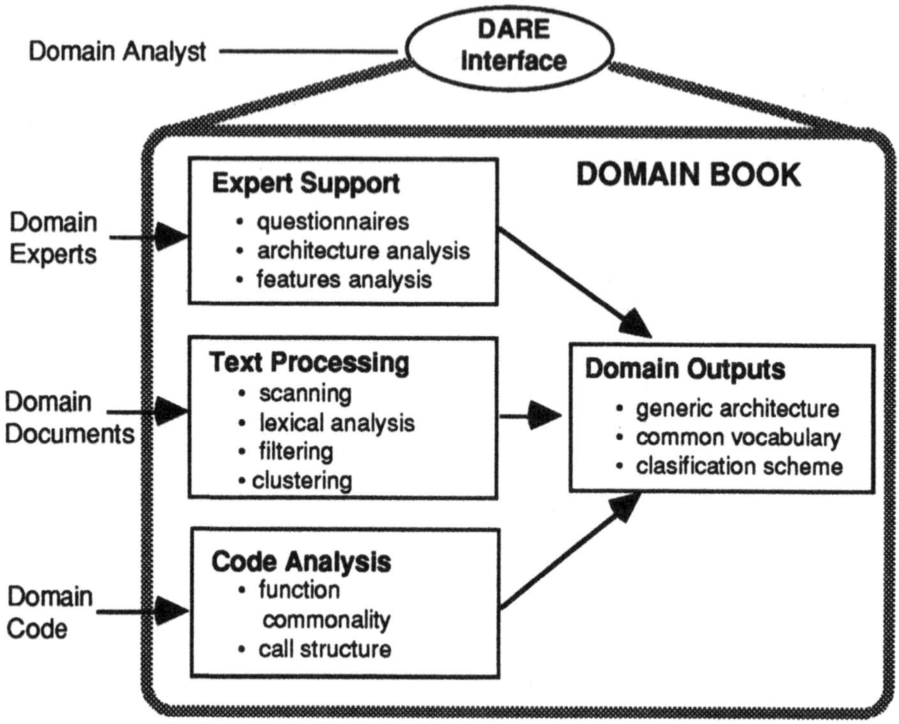

Figure 4 DARE Process Model

7 Conclusions

The proposed new paradigm for software development is based on systematic reuse. It requires the creation of a reuse infrastructure that improves as multiple applications are produced. The reuse infrastructure was compared to an assembly line which is expensive to create but once established it results in substantial production and increased pay-off. A reuse infrastructure evolves but it needs an initial bootstrap. DARE is a promising tool for enabling the creation of an initial reuse infrastructure.

References

1. Prieto-Díaz, R. (1993). Status Report: Software Reusability. IEEE Software, 10(3), 61-66.
2. Griss, M. L. (1993). Software reuse: From library to factory. IBM Systems Journal, 32(4), 548-566.
3. Systematic Reuse, special issue. (1994). W. Frakes and S. Isoda (Eds.), IEEE Software, 11(5).

4. Neighbors, J. (1980). Software construction using components. Ph.D. Thesis, Department of Information and Computer Science, University of California, Irvine.
5. Lanergan, R. G., & Poynton, B. A. (1979). Reusable code: the application development technique of the future. In Proceedings of the IBM SHARE/GUIDE Software Symposium, Monterey, CA, October, 1979.
6. Matsumoto, Y. (1984). Management of Industrial Software Production. IEEE Computer, 16(3), 59-72.
7. Prieto-Díaz, R., & Frakes, W. B. (1992). DARE: A domain analysis and reuse environment (SBIR Phase I Final Report No. Contract# DAAH01-92-C-R040). DARPA/U.S. Army Missile Command, AMSMI-RD-PC-JB-R, Redstone Arsenal, AL 35898-5280.
8. Prieto-Díaz, R. (1991). Reuse Library Process Model (Final Report for STARS Reuse Library Program No. Contract# F19628-88-D-0032). Electronic Systems Division, Air Force Systems Command, USAF, Hanscom AFB, MA 01731.

Planning for Reuse

Jean-Marc MOREL
Bull S.A., Rue Jean JAURES - F-78340 Les Clayes-sous-bois, France.

Abstract

From 1991 the REBOOT consortium and then the SER consortium have investigated the problems of introducing reuse into software producing organisations and developed a comprehensive approach to efficiently address organisational, managerial, and technical aspects of software reuse. The purpose of this paper is to demonstrate a coherent process for introducing reuse into an organisation and to present the fundamentals of a successful reuse policy which stem from the various experiences carried out in various domains throughout Europe.

Keywords: software reuse, software development process, process improvement, business process re-engineering.

1 Introduction

Software reuse represents the most significant opportunity for the software development industry to earn the name "software engineering".

On the other hand, experience shows that sustainable benefits of software reuse arise from improvement programs which address business, organisation and management along with engineering and technology. Indeed, when reuse is understood and managed in a completely organisational context, it becomes aligned with the organisation's software processes to establish a strong, general, underlying trend towards improvement.

In this paper we will sketch the REBOOT approach we have developed from various case studies in different software producing organisations.

First, we will discuss the main obstacle to overcome: How to transform the company for software reuse?

Then, we will show that a complete methodology is needed to help all involved people adopt and practice reuse.

Finally, we will explain how to measure reuse capability and how to build a reuse project plan to ensure a smooth, continuous and efficient adoption of reuse.

Last but not least, reports from two case studies are given in appendix to illustrate the results that can be achieved by applying this methodology.

2 Transforming the Company for Software Reuse

Introducing and harnessing software reuse is a team effort:

- **company managers** must initiate and allocate resources for reuse activities into operational programs.

- **market and business developers** must assess business opportunity and define strategies for reuse in market development programs;

- **development engineers** must adapt their processes to the effective application of reuse methods and technology, while

- **product managers** must direct the growth of the reusable asset base and improve product reaction to market demand.

REBOOT experience shows that effective progress requires all aspects to be managed as a co-ordinated evolutionary process. The spiral in Figure 1 illustrates a phased process for the introduction of reuse into a company. The inner circle describes operation in a narrow business domain, with high development and maintenance costs and slow response to market demand. Casual reuse, not actively supported by the management team, yields minor benefits because the development is product-specific oriented with a narrow focus.

Then, in the second circuit of the spiral, we see the company management initiating organisational changes, adapting the engineering process to reuse, and initiating a pilot experiment. This yields more easily re-configurable products and consequently shorter lead time for further deliveries in the domain. At this stage, the company will also benefit from the existence of a proven reuse capability that can be expanded.

The third circuit of the spiral shows a co-ordinated activity to plan, implement and market into a wider domain.. The reuse-based process becomes the standard for development. Domain analysis and domain modelling techniques are introduced to improve co-operation between market and product development teams. Market performance improves through faster response in bidding and delivering into a wider domain in the marketplace. Further expansion can then be managed.

Of course, each company is unique and has its own characteristics (e.g. market, competition, competence, technology, culture, organisation, and tools).

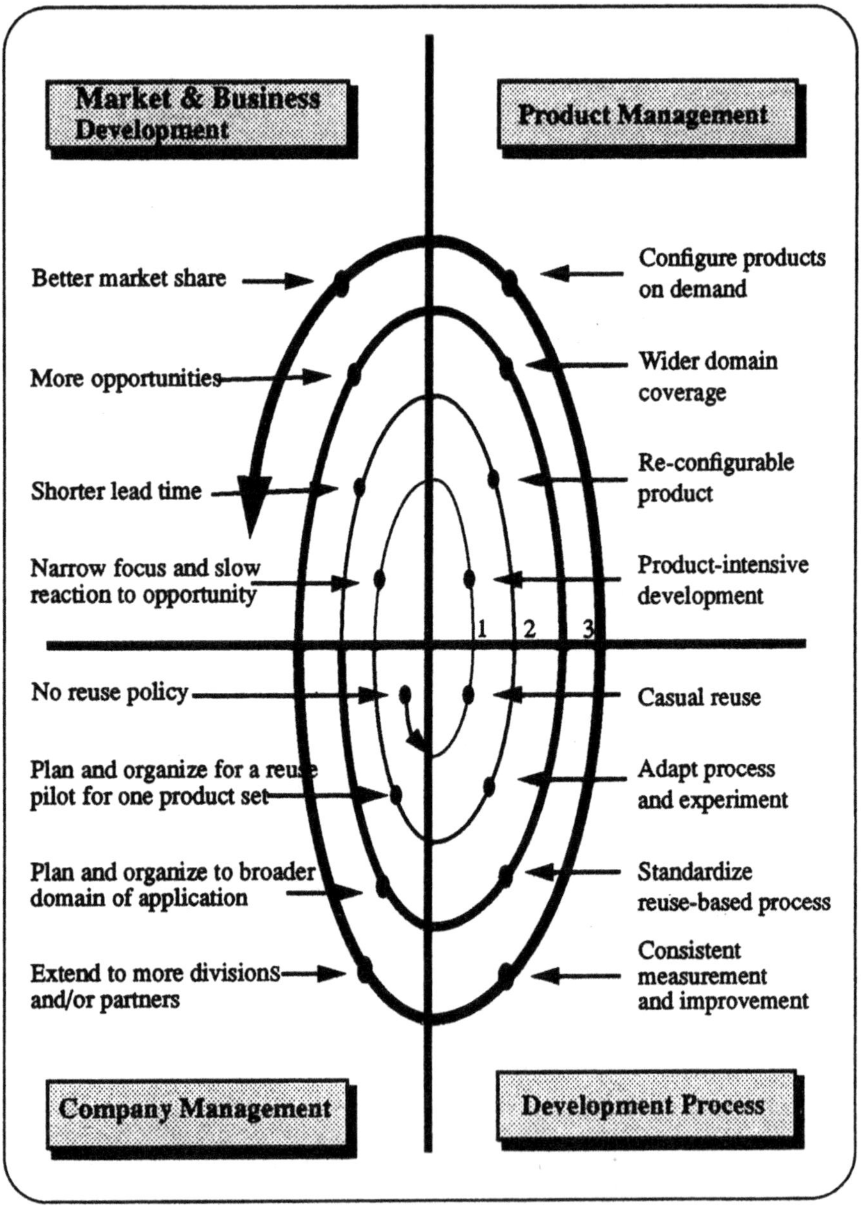

Figure 1 : The reuse improvement spiral

These must be well understood before designing and implementing a reuse program. The REBOOT introduction process does help a company define its strategy for reuse, assess its capability in the various key reuse areas (management, development process, etc.), and plan a consistent set of actions in order to get onto and follow a company-specific spiral.

Experience has shown that, using this co-ordinated approach, the costs are more manageable, the benefits are better valued, and the company is better equipped to re-focus as a cohesive unit in the face of opportunity or threat.

3 The Need for a Complete Methodology

Systematic reuse affects most parts of the organisation and without considering all parts it will have limited success. Once the overall strategy is defined and a set of co-ordinated actions are planned, all actors, from company management through market and product management to engineering people, must also be given guidance and support for day-today implementation of reuse. In other words, a complete methodology is needed which:

- supports the management team to make informed decisions,
- provides process and detailed guidelines both for:
  - developing FOR reuse, that is growing a base of reusable assets;
  - developing WITH reuse, that is developing products by reusing appropriate reusable assets stored in the base;
- helps to integrate these processes into the existing software development process, and
- helps to plan reuse-specific activities, measure costs and benefits of reuse, assess and adapt reuse processes.

The guidelines for this approach are embodied in a complete end-to-end methodology [1] that covers the total software development life cycle as well as organisation, product management, and project management.

Some companies are committed to applying object-oriented techniques, while others believe investments in existing assets must be re-deployed as much as possible. The REBOOT approach applies in both cases and provides a complete support. This has been verified through several application projects in various contexts (e.g. telecommunications, network management, office systems, factory planning, etc.) - See short reports of two reuse case studies in the appendix.

4 Choosing the Building Blocks

The aim is to reuse all possible assets, not only code. Wherever possible, these should be complete packages consisting of specification and design documents, code, test procedures, and all associated knowledge. This is applicable at four levels:

- Basic component, applied in small scale integration.
- Object-oriented framework (or domain-specific architecture), applied to large-scale integration through instantiation of abstract classes and functions by specific implementations.
- Sub-system, applied through its integration into the building of a new application possibly with re-engineering or adaptation of code and interfaces.
- Ready-to-execute application, simply applied through calls.

Development and product management co-operate to identify suitable choices of reusable building blocks, then select the most appropriate engineering processes and technological support. This also contributes to determining how to get onto and follow the spiral described in figure 1.

5 Positioning Products in the Marketplace

An effective way of understanding products in a market context is through domain modelling. This is done by modelling an application domain and then manipulating a range of products or part products within the domain model. This enables the identification of both the extensions needed to meet a wider market opportunity, and the opportunities for reuse of domain-specific building blocks. Used in this way, domain modelling also provides a focused ability for growing the reusable asset base.

6 Growing the Reusable Asset Base

As mentioned previously, we distinguish two essential processes in software reuse engineering (see figure 2):

- **Development FOR reuse**, in which engineers identify what is potentially and profitably reusable, then record related knowledge while designing, qualifying, constructing and classifying software artefacts for reuse in solutions other than those initially targeted.
- **Development WITH reuse**, in which engineers search for, evaluate, adapt and integrate ,existing and appropriate knowledge, specifications, designs, code, tests and documentation to deliver quality products in shorter

time at lower costs. Indeed, these assets can be searched for from the repository (the base of reusable components), but also from other systems developed in the company or from public bases accessed through world-wide networks.

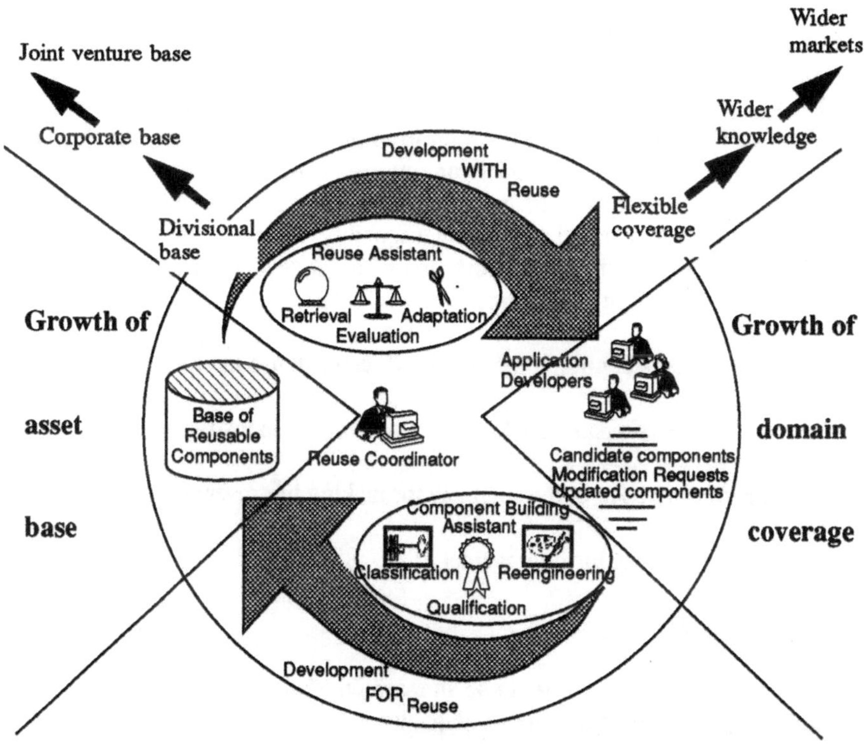

Figure 2 : The Reuse Engineering Diagram

These two distinct methods co-exist to grow the company's reusable asset base and gain the maximum benefit by reusing those assets. Moreover, as suggested in figure 2, there are possible extensions to deploy a departmental or divisional database of reusable assets into a corporate base, or even to establish joint ventures within specific industry sectors. On the other hand, as mentioned earlier, domain modelling first yields flexible coverage of the domain, and then enables better coverage of the whole domain by gaining wider knowledge and ultimately wider markets.

7 Measuring Reuse Capability

The essence of the REBOOT approach is to ensure that all necessarily interdependent actions are taken across an organisation to achieve success.

Measurement is essential to real understanding of a company reuse capability. The maturity model is becoming a recognised way of assessing capability. Derived from the work of Deming, by evolving standard measures in a progressively attainable ladder as a motivator for performance improvement, examples are the SEI[1] Capability Maturity Model and the BOOTSTRAP[2] Model.

The Reuse Maturity Model (RMM) [1] has been developed by the REBOOT project to measure the extent to which a company succeeds in developing, maintaining and using all reusable assets at its disposal. The RMM contains factors that can be worked on to improve the level of maturity. These factors split into five areas: organisation, management, development (FOR and WITH reuse), classification of reusable assets, and metrics. Each factor has a ladder of measures to assess the company capability for the corresponding reuse aspect. An improvement cycle starts with a systematic assessment of the company from which the management and technical team can determine:

- a common understanding of the company's competence in reuse;
- how mature the company is relative to a developing industry norm;
- what options are open to the company for making improvement;
- what priorities to set for improvement;
- what standards to target.

The maturity assessment appears to be an essential planning step for introducing and advancing software reuse into a company.

8 The Reuse Adoption Process

Introducing reuse means incorporating the practice of reuse as a permanent part of a company's culture and way of doing business, that is institutionalising reuse.

As for any software process improvement, the introduction of reuse must be achieved using a stepwise approach such as the IDEAL approach from Carnegie Mellon University which contains five phases: Initiate, Diagnose, Establish, Act, Leverage (hence IDEAL) [2]. Hence, the reuse adoption process we use is as described in figure 3.

---

1 SEI stands for Software Engineering Institute in Pittsburgh - US.

2 BOOTSTRAP is an Esprit project which developed a software development process assessment method.

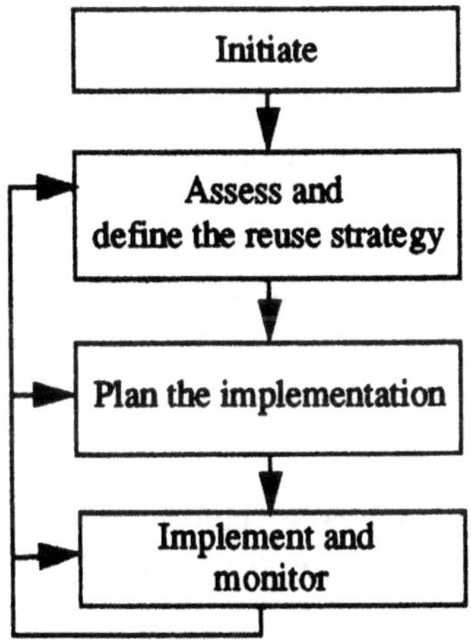

Figure 3 : The reuse adoption process

These various steps can be summarised in the following way:

Initiate means:

- Inform management of technical & organisational aspects of reuse.
- Identify how reuse can help achieve the main objectives of the company.
- Pre-assess reuse opportunities.
- Collect previous reuse experiences in similar contexts.
- Identify other initiatives which can be coupled to the reuse initiative.
- Set up a Task Force to investigate and define the reuse introduction programme and a Reuse Board to supervise and direct the implementation effort.

Assess and define the reuse strategy means:

- Analyse the market of the company in order to discover reuse opportunities -current or potential customers with similar needs.

- Analyse the products of the company in order to discover reuse opportunities within and between product families. Here one must consider restructuring into subsystems & layered architectures as well as portability & independent from technology changes.

- Analyse the current organisation, the development processes and practices (using the Reuse Maturity Model).

- Study how can this organisation, the processes and the practices can be adapted or enhanced to incorporate reuse, and define the appropriate strategy.

Plan the Implementation means:

- Choose, adapt, and plan how to implement the appropriate set of reuse techniques which can best support the chosen reuse strategy.

- Define concrete goals for each key reuse area: Organisation, Project management, Development process, Component management, and Metrics.

- Select pilot projects (analyse opportunities and risks).

- Prepare for training and assistance.

- Organise monitoring.

Implement and Monitor means put into operation roles, processes, methods, and tools that support fruitful reuse, that is:

- Ensure the commitment to, and understanding of reuse in the pilot projects.

- Train, educate, and provide extensive support.

- Follow up, collect and consolidate data to monitor progress.

- Analyse problems and react consequently.

- Disseminate results.

9 Documenting Reuse Implementation

It is acknowledged that a key factor for the success of a reuse introduction programme is good communication; this implies that the reuse adoption process must be carefully described, widely disseminated throughout the software producing organisation in order to keep all involved people well informed of the objectives and of the workplan.

Then, as mentioned above, the implementation must be rigorously followed-up in order to collect feedback and results. Again, it is quite important to regularly report about progress and possible problems both to be able to react and keep people aware of ongoing efforts.

As a spin-off, we frequently observed that such reports contribute to the enhancement of the reuse introduction process and greatly help convince others to start reuse.

The Reuse Project Plan we propose is composed of:

- a short introduction to present the purpose of the report,
- a Part I to describe the overall strategy and plan,
- a Part 11 to describe the objectives, the action plan, as well as corresponding results collected on a regular basis throughout the implementation.
- a Part III to collect cost/benefit data.

10 Conclusion

Implementing reuse in a company is a matter of adopting new ways of thinking and new habits at all levels in the hierarchy. The definition, the institutionalisation, and the measurement of overall software processes in a business context gives the company a realistic context for evaluating, and gaining the full potential for the reuse of software.

Another important point is that the fundamental requirement of software reuse is 'discipline'. Truly, that is what separates software developers from software engineers.

From our experience in various software producing organisations, it is clear that the key factors for success are:

- Managerial involvement.
- Strong technical leadership.
- Efficient communication between teams.
- Explicit integration of reuse activities in development process.
- Effective standardisation of product and process.
- Accurate training and motivation of people.

Acknowledgement
The author wants to acknowledge all partners of the REBOOT consortium[3] who contributed to the development and validation of the REBOOT methodology, as well as all people from external application companies who have experimented with it. Special thanks go to Richard Thomas who helped a lot in describing the overall reuse adoption process at company level.

References

[1] Karlsson E-A (ed.) Software Reuse: A Holistic Approach. John Wiley & Sons, 1995. REBOOT Methodology Handbook.

[2] Radice R. & Peterson B. An Integrated Approach to Software Process Improvement. Tutorial. Pittsburgh, PA: Software Engineering Institute, Carnegie Mellon University, August 1994. The IDEAL Approach.

---

[3] The REBOOT consortium includes Bull S.A. (France) (co-ordinator), Cap Gemini Innovation (France), EP-Frameworks (Sweden), Q-Labs (Sweden), Sema-Group sae (Spain), Siemens AG (Germany), Sintef (Norway) and TXT Ingegneria Informatica S.RA. (Italy).
The REBOOT project (EP7808) was co-funded by the European Commission.

Appendix: Reuse Case Studies

Several application projects in a variety of industry domains were conducted in the life of the REBOOT project. These projects provided a valuable environment for applying, evaluating and refining the methodology. Two of them are reported here to indicate the approach, benefits and major issues experienced.

Case 1: Achieving competitive advantage through reuse in the telecommunications industry

This example is taken from assignments by EP Framework in Sweden with a company producing software for the global telecommunications market place. Software has to be developed for each of the three major markets: Europe, the US and the Pacific region. Many functional aspects of the domain are similar, but each region is influenced by local standards and practices resulting in specialised solution development for clients in geographic regions.

The company recognised increasing competition in a growing market, typified by an increasing number of operators and an increasing number of small specialist suppliers in the marketplace.

Software reuse apparently offered a potential solution to companies working in a changing marketplace, so the company set out to answer the following questions:

- What is the potential for software reuse across the world-wide operation?
- What is the approach to introducing reuse into this type of organisation?
- What are the perceived and actual benefits?

The company decided to investigate reuse

Preliminary estimates from a regional viewpoint concluded that approximately 40% of the source code across the three regions might be reusable. This conclusion justified further investigation.

Systematic analysis of the reusability of requirements based on domain knowledge, design specifications and source code revealed that:

- 90% of requirements were reusable;
- 80% of the design specification was reusable;

- 70% of the source code should be common, and was therefore potentially reusable.

Clearly the potential existed for benefiting from a common base of marketable assets, with a greater focus on applications engineering, rather than on specialised development for regional markets.

The introduction plan

Reuse consultants recognised that introduction of a technically focused activity would, on its own, not achieve the potential benefits. Organisational and management actions would also be necessary to effectively provide a complete reuse solution. The goal was to provide the way of working and the supporting infrastructure that would ultimately lead to regional contribution and access to a common base of reusable software assets. This would inevitably lead to change at the organisational level by redefining some roles and responsibilities.

What results would this give to the company?

Increasing availability of world-wide computer networking facilities makes this type of global operation feasible. The REBOOT vision for this type of company is a way of working that brings:

- a greater concentration of resource to understanding the domain of application - thus increasing revenues through more application oriented business;

- a greater understanding of the world-wide availability of software assets reusable for building solutions - thus shortening delivery time;

- the isolation and minimisation of software which is based on local standards and practices - thus reducing customisation costs;

- the development of reusable components governed by domain knowledge and the acquisition, through surveys across other domains, of additional software for inclusion in the repository - thus increasing the software asset;.

- the configuring of solutions for any application from a common repository - thus widening the domain coverage.

This would bring an ability to supply competitive solutions across the overall marketplace, specialising these to the needs of specific operators and building up the company component base as a value added program.

The core of the improvement strategy

The key to changing the organisation and processes in a consistent manner lies in finding the means of optimising development investment to meet market opportunities. Concentration of upstream effort in developing frameworks to meet known domain requirements can improve product line management and ultimately govern the management of a repository. Accordingly, the pilot project concentrated on the development of a framework to be applied in two applications in one domain.

What has been achieved?

The company committed to an initial program of carefully managed and engineered reuse projects, which demonstrated the following benefits:

- Using the framework co-ordinates requirements of the domain to achieve 90% commonalty against a previous 60%; the components governed by the framework are 50% more reusable.

- Developing one application along with a framework costs 1.4 times the cost of classical development.

- Developing two applications along with a common reusable framework costs 1.75 times (instead of 2 times) the cost of classical development - more than breaking even.

- Developing further applications using the framework reduces to 0.35 times the cost of development from scratch.

- By involving managers and engineers to plan and carefully engineer the reuse aspect of the work, casual or tactical reuse was eliminated - thus improving quality and reducing costs of repair activity.

The company is now confident in continuing an evolutionary program to improve knowledge and competencies and in developing frameworks for reuse in selected product lines. Planning with the intention of reusing any developed framework is clearly essential for benefits to be gained.

Conclusion

The telecommunications company example (case 1) indicates how the extent of such a transformation requires a complete methodology that addresses organisation, management, engineering and technology. Planning involved defining a start point from a realistic and accurate view of the organisation and the way in which it operated at the time, and then defining programs as a series of manageable, evolutionary steps. Planning guidelines were derived from the methodology and customised to the domain of application by the REBOOT consultants.

In short, the methodology was applied in the following way:

- The combined processes of marketing, product management and development were analysed in a corporate management context.

- The organisation was assessed as being ready for reuse, based on the high commonalty of requirements across the world-wide markets.

- The focal point for reuse was identified from which an attainable, evolutionary program could be started.

- Results and new situations to be managed were fed back to redirect the evolution.

- Openness of the methodology allowed local solutions for methods and tooling to be applied.

- The methodology provided the guidelines for the transition and these were customised to the domain of application by the REBOOT consultants.

Case 2: Achieving competitive advantage through reuse in the office-systems industry

The example is taken from experience at Bull S.A. (Paris - France) in producing software for client server based solutions in the office systems marketplace. The operation is aligned to the company's open systems strategy based on the Distributed Computing Model. The activities of the division divides into development of application specific products (e.g. for image processing) and platform related products (e.g. for user interface).

The major motivator for examining the benefit of reuse has been the need for combating increased competition in an ever growing client-server market. This market is typified by high volume software suppliers, an increasing number of small specialist suppliers and a fast rate of change across the typical range of products available to the market.

We will explain how reuse has helped Bull work more efficiently in this changing marketplace.

Why reuse was considered by the division

Initial analysis revealed a good potential for reuse in the division. This view was based on:

- the coexistence of several product streams and several sub-system development streams;
- recognition of the need to deal with a high rate of change in the operating and development systems;
- recognition of the immediate benefit of rationalising the organisational structure to configure products from common sub-systems - thus releasing more resources to product improvement;
- recognition of the potential of the resulting organisation to evolve a reusable component base to be used in product development.

The strategy for introducing reuse

The primary goal was to improve time to market for functional and platform changes. Re-configurable products would be constructed to meet market requirements from a base of reusable components. Improvement would be in flexibility and quality of products, with increased overall productivity.

Workflow systems were chosen as a pilot domain because this field is dependent upon, and builds on, many innovative and emerging technologies. The strategy was first to pilot the introduction of reuse to workflow systems development while involving the image and document processing teams. Then, the resulting reuse technology would be deployed to the entire department, and later, more generally within the company.

What has been achieved

The organisation has been transformed to a way of working in which:

- more resources are allocated to meet the functional requirements of the application domain;
- there is a greater awareness of the need for, and the availability of quality components which can be built into quality products;
- the emphasis is to configure products from a growing base of reusable components; and
- additions to the component base are developed or acquired to meet the identified product requirements of those domains to which the division supplies products.

The effect is a re-balancing between the product and component base to supply competitive solutions across the overall marketplace, specialising these to the needs of the marketplace and building up the component base as a value added program.

The stage of transformation achieved

The view within the division is that the foundation has been laid to really begin to reap benefit from this approach. There is always a need for achieving some degree of critical mass, to arrive at a turning point, after which the major gains begin to be made. In this example, the division:

- has re-focused to exploit reuse.
- identifies, develops, and reuses more common sub-systems,
- is growing a component base.

The cost of transformation

The evidence shows little difference in cost between developing software FOR reuse compared with traditional software development. Consistent use of the REBOOT methodology results in the transformation costs being absorbed in the on-going development programs. Well-planned reuse actions enabled to both institutionalise and control reuse. As a result, the additional costs have been recovered within the development of the first version.

Benefits

The organisation has achieved a balance between product and component development and, as a result, evolves the products and the components in a consistent manner. Significantly less effort is needed for implementation detail and basic technology development. The combined effect of dedicating more effort to providing required product features, and of the availability of suitable components to meet these requirements, is an improved response to market need.

In addition, the organisation has become more focused on configuring products from proven parts and has started to integrate products into other environments.

The overall benefit of this has been to position the company to offer more competitive products supplied in a shorter time. For example, the new version of the flowPATH product offers much more functionality which mostly comes from reuse of large components (e.g.- ImageEditor, Communication layer, ContentPATH). Moreover, other teams in the division as well as product line people have become converted and reuse-minded too. As a result, the overall product line is getting more consistent, compatible and attractive.

Typical experienced cost benefits

In this committed and organised reuse program, experience includes:

- a sub-system, with a development cost of 4 PY (Person-Years), reused 5 times, saving 20 PY.
- a sub-system, with a development cost of 2 PY, reused twice, saving 4 PY.
- a framework, with a development cost of 2.5 PY, reused twice, saving 2 PY each time.
- a stand-alone product whose parts have been reused in another product, saving 0.5 PY.
- a generator, with a development cost of 2 PY, expected to save 4 PY.

The extra-cost for developing these reusable sub-systems and frameworks is about 30% of the normal development cost while costs of reuse are quite low (1-4 Person-Months) compared to the savings.

These benefits continue to grow as the number of projects reusing these well-designed and well tested frameworks and sub-systems increases.

Last but not least, savings in maintenance are also substantial because the shared sub- systems are preserved as a single code base, thus keeping the support costs down to a fraction of what they would be if separate groups had to maintain their specific source code separately.

Lessons Learned

Among the lessons teamed are:

- Reuse in-the-large (reuse of sub-systems) yields more benefits than reuse in- the-small.

- Development FOR reuse, co-ordinated with the development of application specific products, has had a beneficial impact on the architecture: it naturally leads to a clearer abstraction of the developed (sub)system that better supports late changes in requirements. Thus development FOR reuse adds to the quality of the developed application right from the start.

- Developing WITH reuse clearly motivates people to develop new reusable components.

- Market and return on investment must be carefully studied and followed-up. Since the technology is evolving rapidly, some components may become rapidly obsolete.

Reuse Lifecycle:
Essentials and Implementations

Suzanne Robertson
The Atlantic Systems Guild Ltd
11 St Mary's Terrace
London W2 1SU
Phone: 0171 262 3395
email:100065.2304@compuserve.com

Abstract

A successful reuse lifecycle integrates essential reuse processes with a design for implementing those processes. The first requirement is to understand the essential processes for creating, using, maintaining and managing reusable assets. The second is to design an effective way of carrying out those processes. If there were no differences between organisations then the same implementation of the reuse lifecycle would suit everyone. However in reality, reuse lifecycles vary tremendously because of differences in many ethnographic factors like: size, skills, goals, geographical location, customs. This paper makes a practical distinction between the concepts behind reuse and the implementation of those concepts in a given organisation.

Keywords: reuse lifecycle, essential reuse processes.

Background

How can you build high quality, bigger, more complex systems in less time with the same resources? The answer is to take advantage of the resources that already exist by reusing existing pieces of software. The idea of software reuse is to assemble systems from existing components and limit the creation of new software to components that do not yet exist. However, like so many common-sense ideas, software reuse is difficult to put into practice because it requires changes to established processes and attitudes. Software reuse requires a development lifecycle that is built around reusable components.

An effective software reuse lifecycle is one based on the essential processes for creating, maintaining, using and managing relevant, understandable and accessible components. The first step in a reuse program is to understand the concepts represented by these essential processes. The next step is to design a software reuse development lifecycle that implements these essential processes so that they work effectively in your implementation environment. The people, skills, infrastructure, hardware, software, machines and attitudes within your organisation are all part of your implementation environment. Differences will exist between the implementation of your development lifecycle and that of other organisations because you need a lifecycle that is environment specific. But, no matter how you implement the development lifecycle it must contain the essential reuse processes in some form of implementation.

Essential Reuse Processes

Let's stand back and consider the essential thinking [1, 2] behind reuse. The context diagram in Figure 1 summarises the reuse lifecycle in its simplest form.

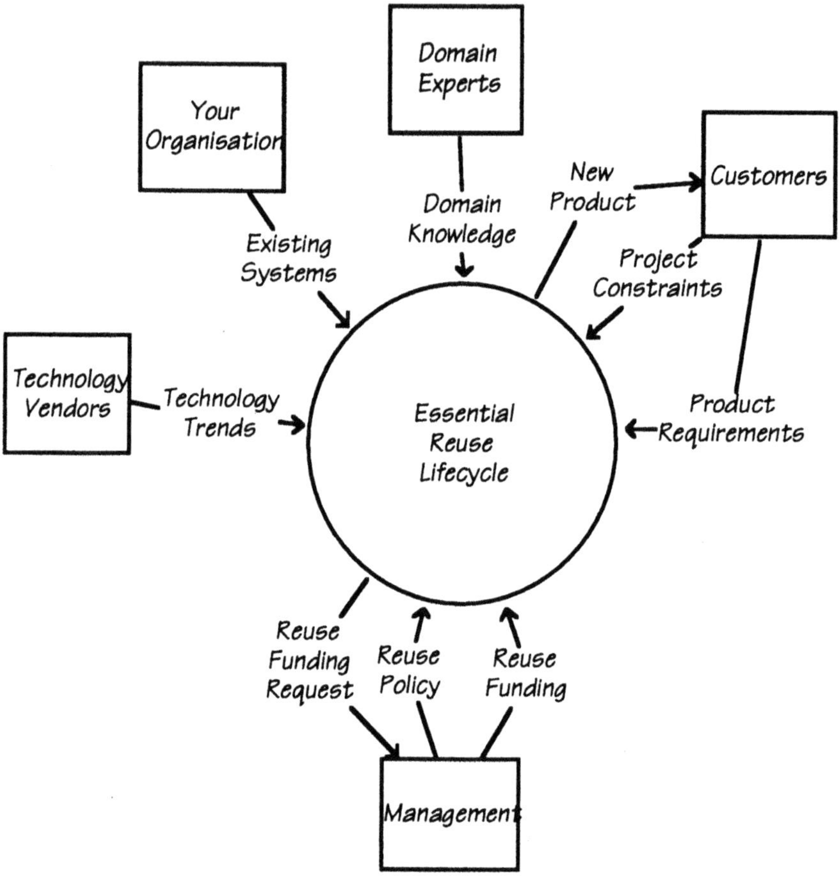

Figure 1: This context diagram summarises the reuse lifecycle by specifying the interfaces with other systems.

Your aim is to produce *New Products* that fulfil the *Product Requirements* within *Project Constraints* of time, cost and quality. Everyone always wants the highest possible quality but this increases the time to produce and the cost of the product. The promise of reuse is to decrease the time and cost at the same time as maintaining high quality. *Domain Knowledge, Existing Systems, Reusable Products* and *Technology Trends*, provide sources for building a library of reusable assets.

Whenever you use an asset from your library, instead of building from scratch, then you make a saving.

Looking at a more detailed view of the reuse lifecycle, we see that the four essential reuse processes [3] are: *Creation, Support, Use* and *Management* of reusable components. Figure 2 illustrates how these essential processes are related to each other by defining the interfaces between the pieces.

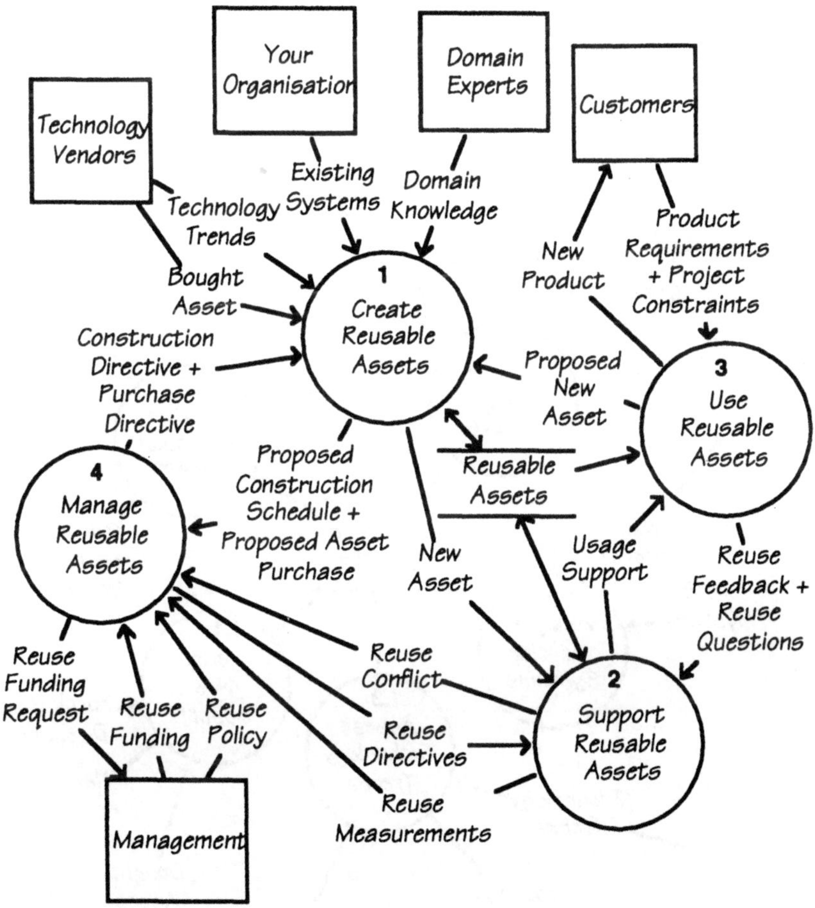

Figure 2: This model of the reuse lifecycle expands the context by showing the interfaces between the essential processes within the reuse lifecycle.

For example, the model tells us that under some set of circumstances the process that uses the assets (Process 3) sends some information about a *Proposed New Asset* to the process that creates the assets (Process 1). Each of the interfaces identifies a dependency between two processes or between a process and another system external to the essential reuse process.

The *Creation* process, illustrated in detail in Figure 3, is a continuous manufacturing process concerned with building a library of reusable assets. The assets might be single components or they might be more complex patterns [4, 5] composed of a number of smaller components. Some of the assets are built from scratch, sometimes in response to a proposal from the users of the assets. Others are derived from existing systems using archaeological techniques. If the reuse marketplace delivers its promise, then the emphasis will shift from in house creation to buying in reusable products.

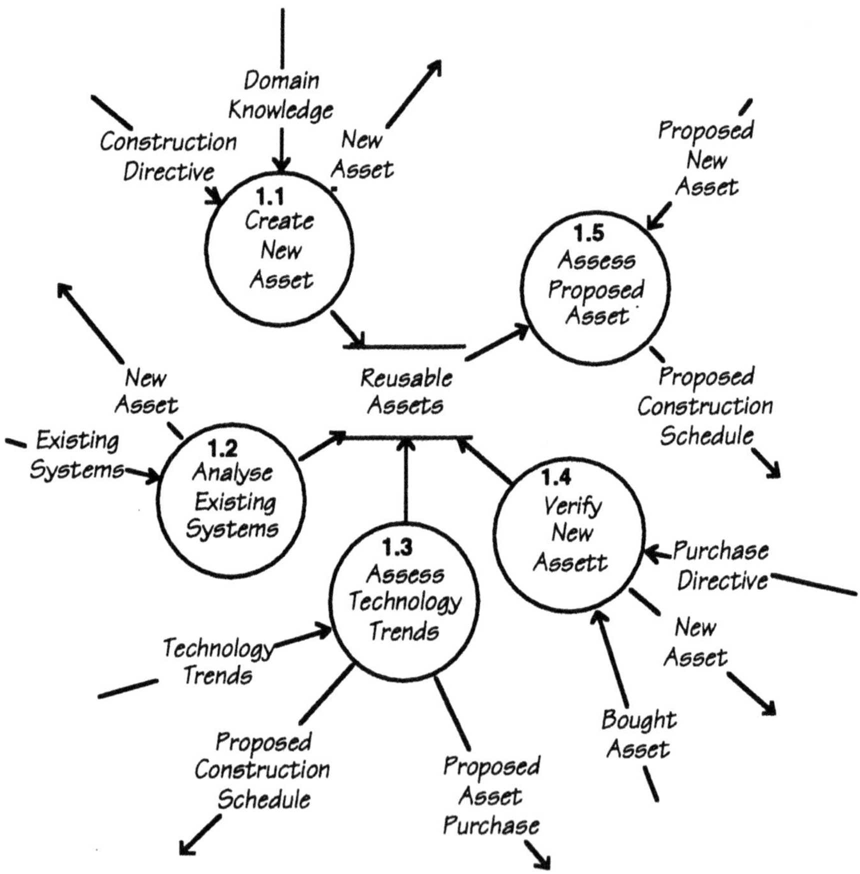

Figure 3: In order to ensure consistency and to have an organisation-wide view, this is the only process that creates reusable assets.

Figure 4 illustrates details of the essential process for the *Use* of reusable assets. Process 3.1 searches the library for assets that match the product requirements. The larger and more diverse the library, the more necessary it is to call on usage support to help in identifying relevant reusable assets. The aim is to build as much of the product as possible using assets that already exist. When a required asset is not found in the library then a proposal for a new asset is communicated to the process that creates assets.

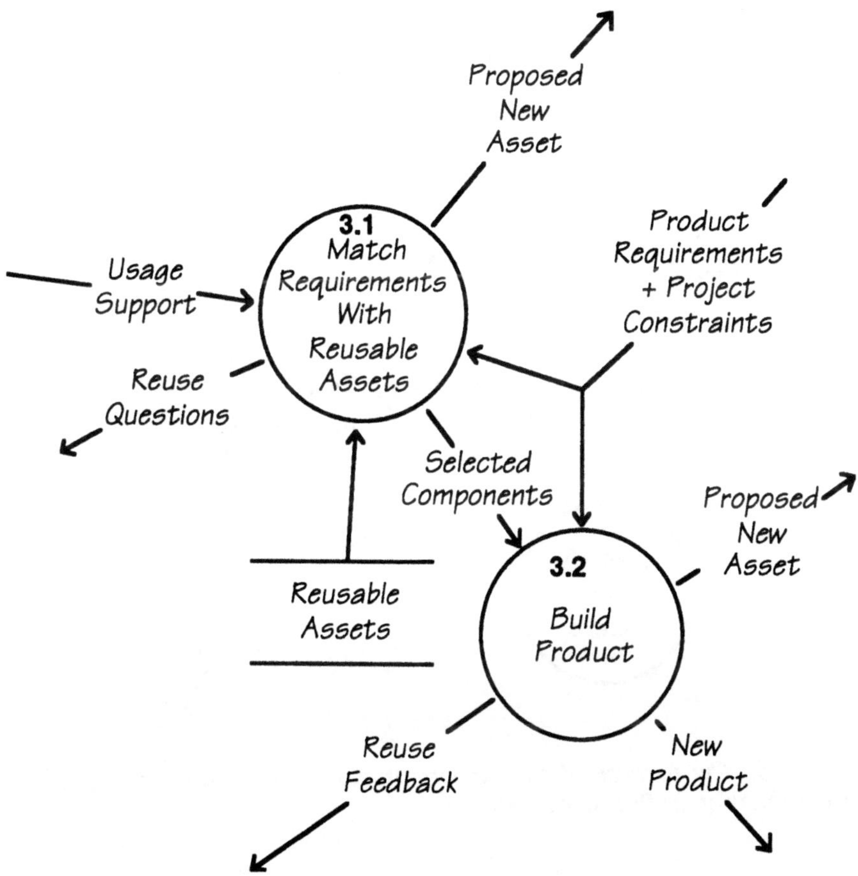

Figure 4: These processes create New Products by reusing assets in the store of Reusable Assets.

The details of the *Support* process are shown in Figure 5. New assets are certified, classified according to the organisation's classification scheme and stored in the library of *Reusable Assets.* The users of the assets ask *Reuse Questions* and the support process uses its knowledge of the library to provide *Usage Support. Reuse*

Feedback from the users of the assets is used to improve the classification of assets, to identify more useful ways of packaging the assets and to provide *Reuse Measurements* for the management process.

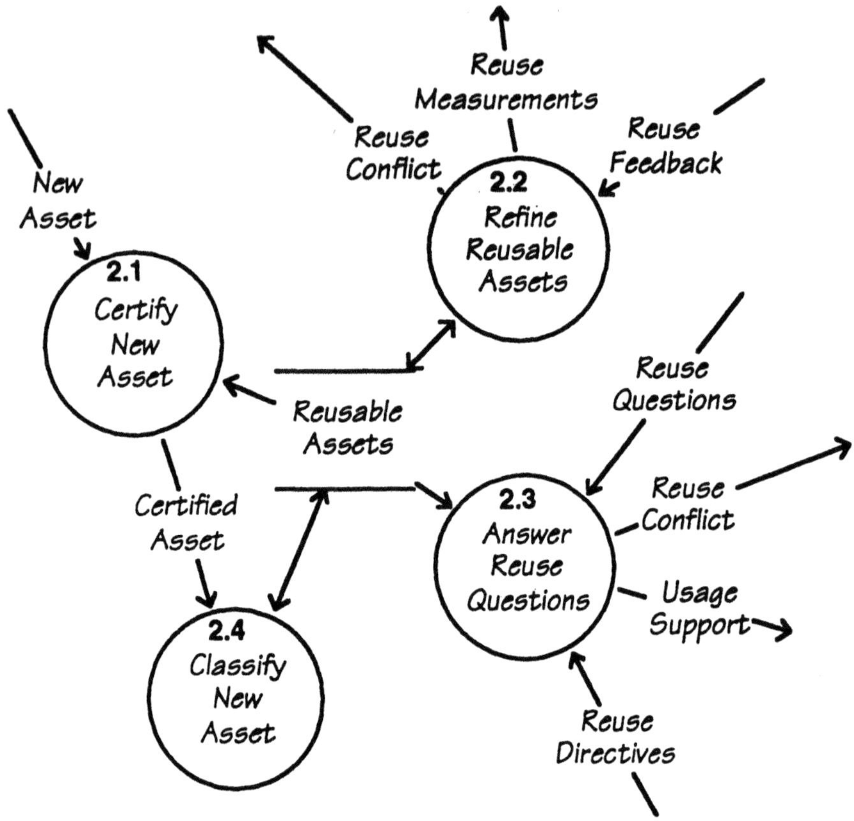

Figure 5: The purpose of the support processes is to ensure the quality and accessibility of the Reusable Assets.

The fourth essential process *Manages* the creation, use and support of the assets. Figure 6 shows how the process plans the creation of new assets, tunes the reuse lifecycle depending on actual experience and resolves any conflicts among the other three processes.

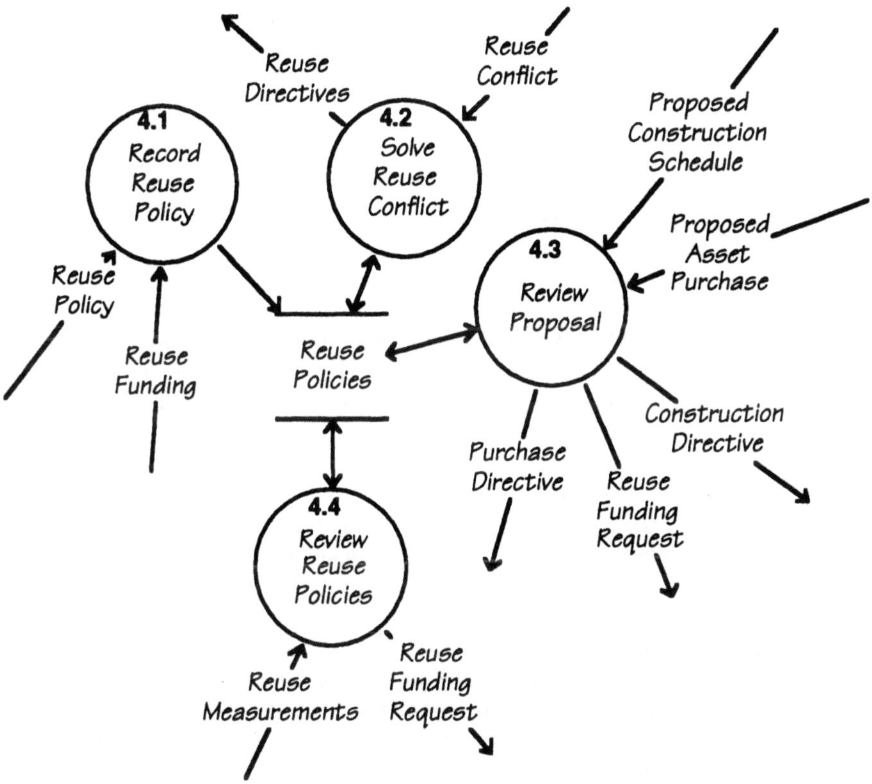

Figure 6: The management processes implement the reuse policy of the organisation and ensure that the business goals are being met.

These four processes identify the essential processes for a reuse lifecyle and the interfaces between those processes. The complete detailed essential reuse lifecycle model would also provide a detailed definition of each of the interfaces (data flows and stores) and each of the processes [1]. For example the store of reusable assets is defined as:

> *Reusable Assets*
> *= {{Reusable Asset Type + Reusable Component + Creation Date}*
> *+ {Reusable Pattern}*
> *+ {Reuse Measurement Type + Reuse Measurement}*
> *+ {Reuse Directive}*
> *+ Reuse Classification Scheme}*

From this we can see that there are many repetitions of reusable component, reusable pattern, reuse measurement and reuse directive and that there is a reuse classification scheme. Each one of the terms would be defined until it can be given a range of values. For instance, the reusable asset type (depending on what types of components you choose to put into your reuse library), could be defined as a list of asset types:

Reusable Asset Type
= [Essential Component
| Organisational Component
| Technological Component
| Constraint Component]

The details of each process would also be specified. For instance, the process *2.1 Certify New Asset* on Figure 5 would be specified to give details of the rules to be carried out when taking a new asset and using information from the store of reusable assets to produce a certified asset.

Remember that the essential reuse lifecycle contains all the things that have to be done independent of technology. Your own reuse lifecycle is a design for fitting the essential lifecycle into your own implementation environment.

Designing Your Reuse Lifecycle

The design for your reuse lifecycle must specify who will carry out each of the essential processes, what technology will be used and how the interfaces between the processes will be implemented. Your aim is to allocate the essential processes to the most appropriate person and technology combination so that you are making the most effective use of your environment.

The ideal design is the one that allocates each essential reuse process to a different person or group of people. The design model would look rather like Figure 2 with the addition of the names of people and technology. This allocation means that the essential processes are not fragmented and each group can concentrate on one functional task that has minimal interfaces to other groups. For instance a group that is only responsible for creation of reusable assets can build assets that are focused towards the organisation rather than just one specific project. This group has the responsibility for keeping track of what is happening in the reuse industry and recommending the purchase of products like class libraries, frameworks and requirements patterns.

The support group is more concerned with the day to day organisation of the reusable assets. This group provides users of the assets with advice and sets up a mechanism for storing and accessing the assets. Perhaps your implementation environment already contains a tool that can be used to store your assets. Or maybe one of the tasks in your lifecycle design is to investigate the products that are currently available for building a reuse library. However it is not always appropriate to automate the storage of all assets.

The Cincinnati Gas and Electric company developed 26 design templates that they reused to implement 350 business events. The support group did not automate these reusable assets. Instead, the accessing mechanism was that the designer would have a meeting with the support group to review the requirements for a business event. The support group would help the designer to select the most appropriate design template. If there was no appropriate template (as often happened at the start of the project) then one was built and given to the support group for quality review and inclusion in the book of design templates. You might find that it is appropriate to store different types of assets in different ways. A guideline is that the more formal your classification and definition of your reusable assets, the more possible it is to automate their storage.

The groups who use the assets are those who are building new products. The aim of these groups is to produce a product within the constraints of the project. And that usually means fast. To make reuse work, a project group must be supplied with appropriate reusable assets, advice on which assets are most appropriate and a mechanism for requesting and receiving new assets. If this mechanism does not work, then the idea of reuse will be little more than lip service and every project group will originate their own code.

Introducing Reuse

A reuse lifecycle is a radical change in the way we build software, and as with any change there will be resistance. When people are expected to change the way they work, they need to understand why the change will be a benefit and how it will affect them. Training sessions help but the most convincing way to nurture the reuse culture is a practical demonstration [6] of the benefits of reuse. Rather than trying to change everything at once, try introducing the concept of reuse on some real work that is being done within the organisation. Start by identifying a problem that could be addressed by using the concept of reuse, look for something that will provide obvious business benefits. Then, using the essential reuse processes and your own implementation environment, design a reuse lifecycle to address the scope of the selected problem. The next task is to apply the lifecycle and use the results as a demonstration of how the reuse concepts have been applied in your organisation. Here is an example of one organisation is applying these ideas.

The Polish Railways are building a new system that involves developers and users at nine different sites [7]. They wanted to share data and, even though the projects are separate, they wanted to reuse the data across all systems. The support group designed a lifecycle to implement the essential reuse processes (see Figure 7), to provide developers with a way of reusing data names and definitions that have already been defined by another project.

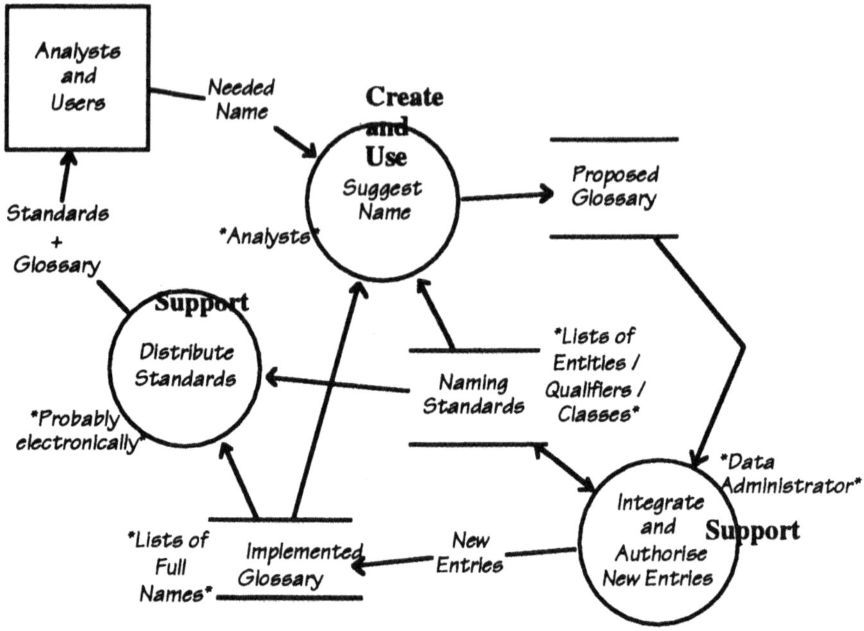

*Figure 7: This model is a design for a lifecycle for creating, using and supporting the reuse of data names. Information about the technology and people that will implement the lifecycle is enclosed in *asterisks*. The* ***bold*** *type identifies which essential processes will be carried out by each part of the system.*

The support group did a high level domain analysis to define a list of names for entities, classes and qualifiers. Whenever an analyst or user on any of the projects requires a name they look in the implemented glossary to see if there is a name that they can reuse. If the name does not exist then the analyst proposes a name using the naming standards. Two of the support group are responsible for reviewing the quality of new names and integrating them into the glossary. The support group are helping the analysts and making them aware that they are already practising reuse and, as a result, experiencing much improved communication between projects.

Conclusion

The design for implementing a reuse lifecycle varies tremendously depending on the people and technology in the implementation environment and the category of asset to be reused. The essential reuse processes, independent of the implementation environment, are an abstraction of the concepts of reuse. All of the essential reuse processes must be implemented somehow, using the facilities available within the implementation environment.

References:

1. Robertson James and Suzanne, *Complete Systems Analysis,*. Dorset House Publishing, New York, 1994.

2. McMenamin Steve and John Palmer, *Essential Systems Analysis,* Yourdon Press, New York, 1984.

3. Griss Martin, *Software reuse: A process of getting organised,* Object Magazine. May 1995. Sigs. New York.

4. Robertson Suzanne, *Reusing The Products Of Analysis,* Second international workshop on software reusability, Position paper, IEEE, Lucca, Italy March 24-26, 1994.

5. Gamma Erich and Richard Helm, Ralph Johnson, John Vlissides, *Design Patterns,*. Addison Wesley, Reading, Massachusetts, 1995.

6. Arango Guillermo, Eric Schoen and Robert Pettengill, *Design as Evolution and Reuse,* Second international workshop on software reusability, IEEE, Lucca, Italy March 24-26, 1994.

7. Lipinski Adam, *Integrating Users With New Techniques When Overhauling A Management Information System,*. Proceedings of the first European conference on software methods. London, October 18-20, 1994.

Reuse: a Cultural Change

Dario de Judicibus
Doctor in Physics
Rome Networking Software Laboratory
IBM SEMEA, Rome, Italy

Abstract

The introduction of Software Reuse in a company is not just a matter of technological change, but of cultural and structural change. In fact, software development is not the only process affected by Reuse. Many other aspects of the life of a company have to be redefined to really take advantage of that discipline. Introduction of Software Reuse in a company is not a painless process. In fact, it requires significant changes to people evaluation, project planning, resource allocation. It may affect social relationships, productivity, quality, the company structure itself. For those reasons, most hindrances to such a re-engineering of a company are social and psychological.

Keywords : Software Reuse, Human Factors, Reuse Process, Individual and Collective Syndromes

Conventions : use of the words *he*, *his*, or *him* in this document should be taken to meant *he* or *she*, *his* or *her*, *him* or *her*.

1 Software Reuse

Reuse in not a new concept in industry. It is, for example, extensively used in the automobile, building, and furniture industry. In the computer world Reuse is the foundation of the hardware industry. However, its acceptance by the Software Development community is still very limited, and only the introduction of Object Oriented Technology (OOT) has given a significant impetus to Software Reuse in most software companies. Nevertheless, the potential advantages of Reuse are often limited by its tight link to OOT. In fact, Reuse is not considered as a valid approach to software development "as is", but just as one of the consequences of using object oriented programming. In many cases, people confuse Software Reuse with Object Oriented Technology, and stress too much the technological aspects of Reuse, rather than the procedural and structural ones.

In fact, Reuse is not a technology, a programming language or a development tool, as well as it cannot be reduced to simply assembling existing code. Reuse is a methodology, and implies the definition of a new process and programming discipline, which have significant consequences on the structure and the culture of a company.

This is at the same time the strongest and the weakest point of Reuse. Once we realize that Reuse is not just a new technology to acquire but a deep change in the way we should work, the return of investment could be really impressive. However, since such an understanding has to bring psychological and social difficulties to account, the diffusion of Reuse in the software community is really scanty.

There are two main problem areas to introduce Reuse in a company. The first one is due to structural problems, the second one is related to human factors. The latter is particularly critical, since overcoming psychological hindrances cannot be obtained by stating the advantages of Reuse from a strictly logical point of view. It is necessary to single out the cares of involved people, and help them to overcome those fears.

Once we get over individual human factors, we have to face the re-engineering of company structures and processes. Such a reorganization may cause social problems due to collective human factors. Hereinafter there is a list of the most common individual and collective reactions to the introduction of reuse in a software company, and some recommendations to solve or limit those problems. However, note that most psychological problems have a well-grounded base on structural and procedural obstacles which often provides a pseudo-logical foundation to individual and collective resistance to Reuse. Therefore, human factors cannot be tackled independently of organization aspects.

1.1 Individual Factors

Individual factors are those that involve the single employee, his fears, his worries, his weaknesses. They are particularly important when the person that is opposing the change is a key person. A manager, a key professional, a person that has to take decisions, and that, therefore, cannot be simply substituted because of his resistance. Those people are often worried that Reuse might limit their position in the company, or might represent a challenge that they cannot face. In most cases this is not true, and the approach to this reaction is to help them understand that the situation is really the opposite. That is, that Reuse will reinforce their position in the company and that it represents for them an opportunity to grow.

The most common individual syndromes are: the **Artist's Syndrome**, the **Standards' Phobia**, the **Egghead's Syndrome**, and the **Feudal Lord's Syndrome**.

1.1.1 The Artist's Syndrome

Most developers consider themselves artists rather than workers. This is mostly due to the intrinsic characteristics of software development. In fact, designing and writing code requires both a good confidence with the technical aspects of programming, and a significant amount of fantasy and intuition. However, the apparent facility in writing code, and the fact that most developers have not a clear understanding of costs of writing lines of code, makes people in software production behave differently from hardware engineers.

For example, an electronic engineer who is designing a new video card for personal computers, does not redesign from scratch all the components of that board, but looks around to identify the best components that are available in the market, and provides the video card with added value by designing new circuits that have not been yet implemented by competitors. During this process he is always very aware of costs, and he does not plan the need for a custom chip unless really necessary. Even in that case, making a new chip is such an expensive approach, that he would prefer to change his design to take advantage of existing integrated circuits, rather than making new ones.

A software engineer often faces the problem to make a new piece of code by designing it from scratch. He automatically accepts the reuse provided by the built-in functions distributed with the compiler, or the class libraries that are included in a C++ package, but rarely does he take the initiative to search for functions or class libraries that are already available inside his company or on the market, and that could facilitate his work.

When a reusable piece of code does not match exactly the requirements of programmers, there is the habit to reimplement that piece of code rather than changing the application design to take advantage of existing software parts. A hardware engineer has no problem to slightly change the design of his card to take advantage of already existing chips, if necessary, because he knows the costs of making a new chip. A software engineer often prefers to sit at his terminal, and make that piece of code from scratch, rather than changing his design. Costs are the manager's business, not the programmer's.

How can we avoid this problem? There are three aspects to consider. The first is purely psychological, the second is cultural, and the third is structural.

First problem: programmers are worried that reusing parts may limit creativity, forcing them to be just assemblers of already existing code, rather than artists. This problem can be eliminated if we present Reuse as a way to take programming to a higher level of abstraction. We could remind programmers that when they moved from machine languages and Assembler to high level languages as FORTRAN, Pascal, or C, they did not give up the pleasure of programming, nor did they give up their creativity. They just stopped reimplementing well-known algorithms to concentrate on a higher level, delegating to built-in functions the most common functionalities.

The concept of built-in operations became larger to include file I/O, string operations, printing, and so forth. Later on, several compilers provided their own extension to the standard libraries, including math libraries, 2D graphic functions, window interfaces, and so on. This introduces us to the second problem: dependencies and support.

The main reason for programmers to naturally accept reusable parts when they are shipped with their favourite compiler, but not from other sources, is that they had already accepted that product as a dependency, and they trust the support provided by the supplier. Convincing a developer to change compilers is not that easy. On the other hand, programmers do not rely on parts that are provided by various organizations or by other developers, even if in the same company, unless there is guaranteed support. And this takes us to the third problem: organization.

Most software companies are organized to associate each development group to a specific project, intended to make profit by developing a product for the market. A group that would develop reusable parts only for other development groups in the same company is considered a cost-only unit, as well as research groups. There is still a culture in many companies that consider those cost-only groups a luxury, not a necessity. So, when Reuse is introduced in a company, many managers try to push product development groups to produce parts, rather than creating Reusable Part Centres. But a development group tightly coupled to a product cannot provide the level of support and responsiveness that is required for reliable, reusable parts.

Therefore, the Artist's Syndrome is mostly a psychological problem, but it is based on the lack of appropriate modifications to the company processes and organization, which weakens the confidence of programmers in reusable parts.

1.1.2 The Standards Phobia

Standards are the foundation of Reuse. Reuse implies that you can assemble parts that have been independently developed in different moments by different programmers. That may cause serious problems of inter-operability. Standards are a necessary even if not sufficient condition to avoid side-effects when assembling parts. In hardware, standards ensure that a video card developed by a company can be used inside a computer made by another company. They ensure that in most cases you can buy your computer's monitor independently from the computer brand you choose. Hardware standards are recognized such an important aspect of hardware production that imposing a standard to the market is a success for a company. Everybody in computer world has heard of IDE, ISA, PCI, VGA, PCMCIA, and so forth.

Software standards exist. They are often the result of the effort of large international communities or company foundations, or invented by a single company operating often in a very specific market. Names like CUA, TWAIN, CORBA, TrueType, OLE, PostScript, and so forth, are well-known among programmers. However, standardization is often seen by many developers as a limitation to their creativity. Imposing standards in a company is difficult. You may ask developers to use certain naming conventions or to use a specific compiler, but many people will mumble if you ask them to use a specific programming style for writing code, or to follow well-defined rules when defining new classes. In fact, whatever standard you may define, somebody will stress the weak points that are always present in any product of the human brain. It is difficult to make people understand that an imperfect standard is better than no standard since developing software is not a technological problem, but an industrial one.

This phobia should be fought by planning a company-wide campaign to advertise the necessity and the advantages of standards. It is necessary to motivate managers to push company standards in their groups, to motivate developers to use them, and to set up an education plan to disseminate the usage of standards among programmers. The availability of tools and products which help programmers to write code that conforms to the company standards will further facilitate their diffusion among programmers.

1.1.3 The Egghead's Syndrome

For many people, knowledge is power. To be an expert is a position to safeguard. Many experts do not like to share their skill with others because they are worried that sharing skills may reduce their importance in the company. Reuse is based on skill sharing and skill encapsulation. Sharing, because Reuse requires artefacts to be made independent of specific people to become a company property. Encapsulation, because properly made reusable parts can encapsulate solutions that are obtained by an expensive and time consuming analysis, so that these parts are available also to non-experts through an easy-to-use interface.

Most eggheads are freelance, wild geese, people who do not like to work with others. The Egghead's Syndrome can be fought by creating a teamwork mentality in the company, by awarding those who share their skill and help others to grow. This problem can be drastically limited by introducing tutoring and mentoring in the company. That would also help to make newcomers feel at ease in the company, increasing the harmony and enthusiasm in each group.

1.1.4 The Feudal Lord's Syndrome

Many managers and team leaders think that their importance in the company is measured by the number of people and projects they manage, by the budget that they received, and in general by the resources with which they have been entrusted. Reuse allows a simplified organization, where large projects are carried out by smaller numbers of people, with significant saving in costs, time, and resources. So Reuse is sometimes seen as a potential danger to the personal career of managers and professionals.

Furthermore, Reuse creates dependencies on other development groups, and in general a good integration of each group in the company mechanisms. That is seen as an interference in the manager's area of control, too.

Even in this case the answer is pushing teamwork culture in the company. Furthermore it is necessary to clearly uncouple the employee position from the amount of resources that he manages. Vice versa, company should award those people who obtain significant results with a few resources.

1.2 Collective Factors

Collective factors are those which belong to the company culture, which is often partly originated by the social structure of the country were the company operates. For example, the **"Not Invented Here" Syndrome** is mostly unknown in Japan. Other syndromes are the **"Technology" Syndrome** and the **"Revenue" Mania**.

1.2.1 The "Not Invented Here" Syndrome

Some companies create in employees a culture of undervaluation of what is done by competitors. *What a competitor does is "surely" inferior to what we do. We can do better. We do it better.* Many employees do not even know the competitor's products. They are not motivated to use them, or at least to give a look at other products.

Such a culture rejects the possibility to reuse whatever was invented by other companies. People reinvent the wheel only to demonstrate that their wheels are better than the others'. This is done even when no license or royalty is requested to take advantage of somebody else's ideas.

This approach is often so deep-rooted that people become distrustful at what is produced by other people in the same company. An internal competition arises with the consequence of a useless duplication of efforts rather than a better production quality. At the moment, in fact, most of the efforts are intended to demonstrate that what is done by others is worse, rather than what is done by us is better.

This syndrome can be cured by introducing in the company a *Culture of Respect*. Respect for competitors, respect for the professionalism of colleagues, respect for each other. Managers should invite their programmers to Vitality Sessions where competitors' products are shown and discussed. The objective must be to identify the weak and strong points of company's product with respect competitors', and to identify which actions could be taken to improve our own product.

1.2.2 The "Technology" Syndrome

When a new methodology, process, or technology is introduced for the first time in a company, it may not deliver its expected advantages immediately. It takes time to tune a new process.

So, especially at the beginning, the process itself is considered responsible for failures. The first OO project resulted to be more expensive than an equivalent "classical" project? Well, it is obvious that OOT is not such a good technology as advertised. A program based on class libraries is more difficult to maintain than good old procedural code? It is technology's fault! Very few people would accept the fact that most of the initial failures are due to themselves, that is, are due to the fact that the used process is still a hybrid of old and new ideas. For example, object oriented languages used as "advanced" procedural languages, classes based on procedural design rather than object oriented analysis, reusable parts that are badly documented, or that do not conform to the same standards.

A new technology might require deep changes in the way we work. A new methodology like Reuse can require deep changes in the way we think, too. To avoid that, it is necessary to carefully select a number of pilot projects led by people who are very flexible and aware that the first attempt to reuse code cannot deliver the results that Software Reuse promises in the long term. Those projects should give the possibility to simultaneously measure and tune the new process, and to demonstrate that reuse is possible. It is also necessary to create a culture that looks at technologies as just tools, which cannot be responsible for human errors, and therefore used as scapegoats when something goes wrong.

1.2.3 The "Revenue" Mania

Companies tend to classify their departments as revenue makers or cost-only departments. For example, a research department is often considered a cost-only department. When a company has financial problems, cost-only departments become natural candidates for cuts. In some companies this approach is so dominant, that when a department requests a service from another one, it is debited as a cost (internal money).

Software Reuse tends to differentiate development groups as *Reusable Part producers*, and *Application builders*. The reason is that a development group that produces reusable parts cannot be tightly coupled to a specific product, because it would be heavily influenced by the perspective of that product. So, Reusable Part Development Centres are intrinsically cost-only departments.

Many managers are hesitant to create a larger number of cost-only departments than those which are considered revenue departments. That is caused by a mentality that is not able to see the company as a whole. They look at the company background as a bunch of independent units which, in the best of cases, are requested to cooperate. This approach is strengthened by the *Feudal Lord's Syndrome*. Often the company becomes an abstract concept, and each single department is individually evaluated, for what it provides in terms of immediate revenue, rather than for the contribution to the company revenue. The larger the company, the stronger is this mindset.

The solution is to make each employee feel as a member of the company, rather than of a specific department or group. The company organization should be seen simply as a necessary decomposition of the whole to better manage the structure. An organization that can also continuously change, according to the change of the external world. In addition, it is necessary to set up a metric to provide a measurable evaluation of cost-only departments in terms of equivalent revenue, so that their contribution to the company can be clearly understood by everybody, and so that they do not become natural candidates for cuts when the company has financial problems.

Conclusion

Any major change to the way people work in a company involves psychological barriers, at individual and collective levels. Those barriers must not be underestimated, because the success of a company to change depends on how much its employees trust the change. Furthermore, none of those psychological barriers is a personal problem only. Most of them have a solid foundation in company structure. This should be addressed to diminish resistance to change.

The introduction of Reuse in a software company is a major change. That cannot be painless, and requires a significant effort by many people. Reuse is by definition a teamwork based approach to development, based on cooperation and a good functioning of company logistics. Just as a worker in any industry cannot have good productivity if the machine maintenance is poor, a product development group cannot have good productivity if the importance of their support services is underestimated.

Reuse divides software development into two areas: part producers and part consumers. Part producers are no longer a production unit, but a logistic one. This has a profound impact on company culture. If human factors are not considered or are underestimated in this cultural and structural change, software reuse will remain an unreachable objective for the company.

Acknowledgments

I would like to acknowledge the terrific support that all the members of the *IBM Reuse Technology Support Center* gave to me in the last few years. In particular, I would like to thank Rock Angier, Peter Drescher, Ian Glass, Hal Gregorius, Bob Heine, Dave Livesey, Slavko Malesevic, Ev Merritt, Jeff Poulin, Norm Rudikoff, Sam V Sultana, Jesus R.Tirso, Thomas Wappler, and Kathy Yglesias. It was really a pleasure to work with them. A special thank to Giampaolo Soleri for his management support, and to Gil Arnold and Marjan Sarshar for help in improving the present paper.

Reuse Measurement & Assessment

Marjan Sarshar
School of Computing & Mathematical Sciences,
Liverpool John Moores University,
Byrom Street, Liverpool L3 3AF
Tel: 051- 231 2320 Fax: 051- 207 4594
Email: cmsmsars@livjm.ac.uk

Abstract

Measuring reuse serves two purposes: *(i)* it quantifies the reuse program and the reusable artefacts, and *(ii)* it assists in improving and encouraging the practice of reuse. *"You can not control what you can not measure"* is the essence of the first purpose. Reuse is a new technology, which dictates multi-dimensional changes to traditional software development. The latter purpose ensures that this transition is successful. Consequently this paper aims to address two questions: *(i) "What to measure?"* , and *(ii) "How can we use measurement for incremental reuse process improvement?"*. The paper takes a goal oriented approach and asserts that there are two sets of reuse goals in any organisation. The first emanates from top level business goals. The second from generic reuse process requirements, which are reflected in Reuse Maturity Models (RMMs). By combining these two approaches, measurements can provide favourable process improvement statistics.

Keywords: Reuse Maturity Models, Reuse Measurement, Goal Question Metrics.

Introduction

Measurement is the process by which numbers or symbols are assigned to attributes of entities in the real world in such a way as to describe them according to clearly defined rules.

There is a degree of confusion surrounding the terms metrics and measure. There are also attempts to distinguish between the notions of metrics and measure. Thus I shall try not to use the term metrics at all because of its different meaning to different people.

In software there are three classes of entities whose attributes we may wish to measure [4] :

Processes: which are any software related activities; these normally have a time factor. This means that they could simply be a time slice of any software project. Examples of processes include reasonably well-defined and coherent activities like that of : constructing a specification document or developing a software system from requirements capture, through to release to customer. Also considered as processes are time slices which do not correspond to any coherent software activity like: The first two weeks of January 1996.

Products: which are any artefacts, deliverables or documents which arise out of the processes. Examples include specification and design documents at various levels of detail, representations of the source or object code, and test strategy documents.

Resources: which are the items which are inputs to processes. Examples include personnel (individual or teams), materials (including offices), tools (software, hardware) and methods. An attribute which is relevant to all these types of resources is cost. In the case of personnel as a resource, in addition to cost, we are especially interested in the attribute productivity.

Measurements are traditionally used in software development to either quantify an attribute, or to predict an attribute. The introduction of reuse, however, requires significant changes to the organisational structure and software development culture. There are two major barriers to initiating reuse under existing organisational practices. Firstly, reuse shifts costs from "producers" to "developers". This has to be accounted for. But an organisation's existing accounting procedures may not be able to handle the different cost elements effectively.

Secondly, the benefits of reuse are long term. However, project managers are generally under heavy time pressure to deliver their products, and can not be expected to respond favourable to a request to invest the added resources necessary to produce reusable software.

In a comprehensive measurement program it is no longer adequate to simply measure product attributes, such as how many times an artefact has been reused. We need to use measurement to ensure that suitable processes are evolving to support and encourage the practice of reuse.

However, measuring process improvement often requires "measuring the un-measurable". To overcome this barrier the technique of process assessment is used in conjunction with measurement.

Approach

This paper proposes that a combination of step by step incremental improvement based on Reuse Maturity Models (RMMs), in conjunction with a Goal Question Metrics (GQM) [2] paradigm ensures that suitable changes are adopted to nourish reuse. This is approach is shown in figure 1.

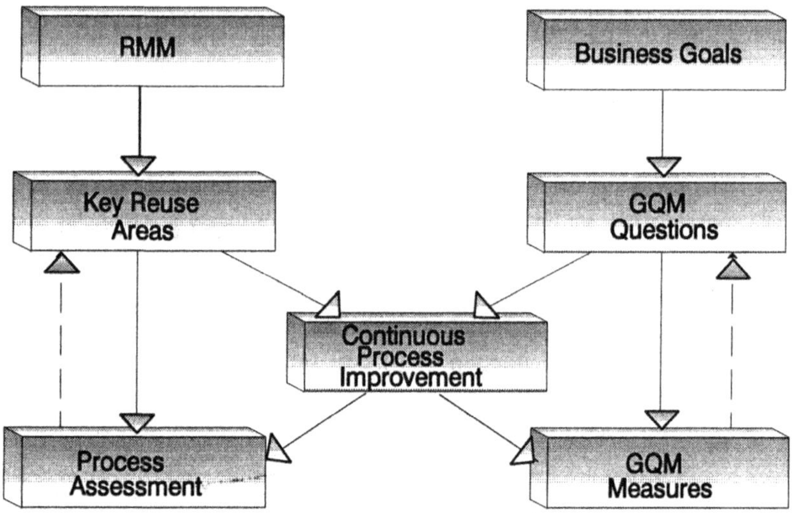

Figure 1- A combination of RMM and GQM approach for improving reuse adoption.

In figure 1, RMM provides a set of generic requirements for reuse programmes, while GQM ensures that corporate goals are considered. Using the GQM paradigm, business goals lead to GQM questions, which direct an organisation to the required GQM measurements. The organisation then decides what to measure, when and how, by analysing the business processes, in the "continuous process improvement" box. Appropriate processes perform the measurements in the "GQM measures" box. These measurements identify which areas demand further attention. "RMM" is broken into more detail by listing the "Key Reuse Areas" (KRAs). These KRAs are assessed, again identifying processes which require further attention. The "continuous process improvement" box in the centre of the figure ensures that the improvements based on RMM and GQM are co-ordinated.

In the next section, the GQM paradigm is introduced and adopted for a reuse environment. In the subsequent section we introduce the concept of reuse maturity models and discuss how they can be used to help stepwise reuse process improvement.

The GQM Approach

The Goal/Question/Metric paradigm (GQM) of Basili [2] is a well known framework for a wide spectrum of software measurement activities. The paradigm provides an informal mechanism for addressing the many kinds of problems which people feel they might be able to help solve through measurement. The idea is that any software measurement activity should be proceeded by the identification of a software engineering *goal* which leads to *questions*, which in turn lead to actual *measurement*.

Corporate Goals

Reuse programs can be mounted for a variety of benefits. It is important to establish the business objectives and provide a structure for a goal oriented approach to the reuse program. A key issue could be time-to-market, or quality, or portability or compatibility with other applications. Perhaps the organisation produces many variant products.

The reuse objectives should be clearly defined, and relate the expected benefits to the business need. Possible benefits include one or more of: *Productivity improvements; quality improvements; timeliness of delivery (time-to-market); Standardisation of technical components; Interoperability & compatibility; New business opportunities; etc.*

It is important not to measure everything, but only the factors which are critical to the success of the business and the plan. The goals listed need to be prioritised, to focus on the most essential objectives.

Reuse Participants

Participants in a reuse program are generally different to the participants in a traditional software development program. Each participant has a different view on how the *goals* can be achieved and what *questions* to pose.

The main participants in a reuse program are the: (i)developers; (ii)consumers; (iii) librarians; and (iv) reuse managers.

Barnes [1] underlines that the activities that work to increase reusability are called *reuse producer* activities and activities that seek to reduce costs through reuse are called *reuse consumer* activities. Vendors of commercial software achieve net cost benefits only when their products are purchased (reused) enough times to cover development costs, just as *reuse producers* achieve a net benefit only when their work products are reused enough times to cover investment costs. Most *reuse producers* (vendors) and *reuse consumers* (buyers) differ from their commercial counterparts primarily in that the transfer of products between them takes place within a single company or project, rather than across company or organisational boundaries. *Reuse producers* and *consumers* introduce the first two views in a reuse program.

To reuse a software component, the consumer must first find it. One of the essential problems in reusing software components is locating and retrieving them from a large collection [6]. Reusable components are held in libraries and managed by *librarians*. The view of the *library managers* is the third view in the reusability process.

Systematic reuse requires long term, *top down management support*. One of the most significant inhibitors of reuse in the software industry is a lack of incentive strategies to encourage co-ordinated reuse investments. Without such strategies, reuse becomes a scavenger hunt, where each reuse customer must bear the full cost of finding, understanding, and modifying work products to meet his needs [1]. The *managerial* view provides the fourth perspective in the reusability process.

Various levels of management have different inputs into the reuse process. Development managers are more focused on the product. Middle managers concentrate mainly on processes & resourcing. Senior managers provide objectives and direction.

Applying GQM

Each category of participants in a reuse program has a different perspective on the program and will pose different GQM questions, based on the goals stated in stage one [Sarshar 94]. These questions lead to a number of measurements. We will demonstrate this approach through a case study:

An organisation indicates that *improving software* quality is one of its major goals. Each participant in the reuse process forms questions to meet this goal. Measurements are listed for each question. An example is provided below:

- the producer

Q: What are the characteristics of a good quality reusable component?
M: component size
M: usability of documentation
M: number of comment lines, etc.

- the consumer

Q: How does the evolution of reused components affect the design in terms of quality?
M: percentage of reuse
M: its affect on number of bugs
M: its affect on reusability, etc.

- the librarian

Q: How do we quality assure library components?
M: number of reuses required to produce "industrial strength" components

- the management

Q: Are there any cost reductions in configuring systems from higher quality reusable assets?
M: cost of producing reusable components
M: cost or reusing these components
M: percentage of reuse

The participants list appropriate measurements for products, processes and resources. Finally, the organisation decides who will measure what, how and where.

The GQM approach indicates effective measurements. However, the success of the measurement programme relies on ensuring that adequate processes exist to support the programme. RMM ensures that correct processes are in place.

Reuse Maturity Models

Reuse adoption processes are, to some extent, based on Reuse Maturity Models (RMMs). A reuse adoption process is a set of guidelines for establishing reuse programs. The RMM models attempt to quantify an organisation's capability to consistently and predictably produce higher quality reusable artefacts and processes.

Risk and cost are usually reduced by starting with a small pilot project, and proceeding incrementally to expand the scope as the reuse process matures. In some other cases, however, the project can not succeed without a significant investment and effort to do major system redesign and implementation. The key idea is to get some early success, and understand the organisational and infrastructure issues that typically impede reuse programs. The importance of early success in order to gain and retain management and engineer buy-in and support can not be overstated.

The "Management and Technology Transfer" working group at the 5th Annual Workshop on Institutionalising Reuse (WISR'92) [5] explored management commitment and support, resources in the form of people, money and time, identifying and planning for organisational changes; changes to the organisation reward structure to help address the motivation issue, measures, investment in technology and team building. They identified three major stages when introducing reuse:

i- *Introduction- Commitment to try reuse:* Focus on technology transfer, learning and feasibility study, and starting a pilot project. Expect to encounter and handle resistance.

ii- *Institutionalisation- Commitment to change and expand the pilot program:* Reuse is integrated into the development cycle.

iii- *Sustain- Commitment to sustain and improve:* The organisation now has a foundation for continuously improving and optimising the process.

Each level includes key reuse areas (KRAs) that identify where an organisation must focus to raise software process to that level. These are listed below.

i- Introduction- Commitment to try reuse:

- determining the domain bounds;
- recommending software reuse process;
- selecting a domain analysis process and a business model.

ii- Institutionalisation- Commitment to change and expand the pilot program:

- facilitation, education and support;
- selecting tools, and technology;
- gathering measurement;
- record and report on progress and lessons learned;
- communicate, motivate people and maintain project momentum through personal contact.

iii- Sustain- Commitment to sustain and improve:

- collecting information;
- providing support and consulting;
- assessing and optimising the reuse producer and consumer processes and expanding the scope of the program.

Other reuse researchers have proposed other more complex models. Karlsson [Karlsson 95] offers an RMM which is then closely tied to the SEI's Capability Maturity Model (CMM).

Using RMM to Achieve Incremental Improvement

The RMMs are based on the assumption that major reuse problems and, hence, causes for software reuse failures are managerial, rather than technical. The RMMs apply process management and quality improvement techniques to reuse implementation and therefore model organisation process improvements.

RMM can be the basis for introducing *incremental* improvements to reuse processes. An organisation seeking to monitor its progress can set *stepwise refinement goals* to achieve a higher level of RMM. The author has not sighted any references to an organisation using RMMs systematically for this purpose. Instead the KRAs are generally used to set a vision for how to improve the reuse process.

Motorola [3] have reported successful stepwise improvements against SEI's CMM by deploying an internal progress assessment mechanism. This paper adapts this approach to achieve incremental reuse refinement.

Key Activities Identification

The KRAs listed above have some common features [Karlsson 95]:

- *Goals*. This describes the goals which the KRA must achieve.
- *Commitment to perform*. This describes the actions the organisation must take to ensure that the process is established and will endure.
- *Ability to perform*. This describes the preconditions that must exist in the project or organisation to implement the software process competently.
- *Activities performed*. This describes the roles and procedures necessary to implement a key process area.
- *Measurements and analysis*. This describes the need to measure the process and analyse the measurements.
- *Verifying implementation*. This describes the steps needed to ensure that the activities are performed in compliance with the process that has been established.

Based on these common features we can list a number of key activities required to achieve each of KRA. For example, at level two of process maturity, the first KRA is "facilitation, education and support". The key activities to achieve this can be listed as:

- *Goals*

1- Facilitation, education and support activities are planned.
2- Reuse facilitation education and support, both organisational and technical are provided.
3- Individuals in the company received the necessary facilitation, education and support.

- *Commitment to perform*

4- A documented policy explicitly specifies the facilitation, education and support required.

- *Ability to perform*

5- Skilled teams of reuse facilitators, educators and support exist.
6- Training programmes for reuse have been developed.

- *Activities performed*

7- Projects are launched with specific role for the facilitators.
8- Project and company education covers reuse.
9- Company wide support is provided for reuse.

- *Measurements and analysis*

10- Measurements of training and support offered, per customer are available.

- *Verifying implementation*

11- The role of the facilitators and support staff are formally reviewed with the project managers.

Assessment Criteria

For incremental improvement, each key activity is assessed against a pre-set evaluation criteria. Appendix A shows an example of evaluation criteria which can be used in a reuse process. All three evaluation dimensions included in this scoring matrix are equally weighed. You determine the score for a key activity by examining all three evaluation dimensions and their scoring guidelines simultaneously. A scoring of 1 represents a poor performance, while 5 represnts an excellent performance.

Internal Evaluation

The key activities of each KRA are rated internally, against this criteria as shown in figure 2.

KRA: Facilitation, education and support List of Activities:		Scoring
1.	Facilitation, education and support activities are planned.	4
2.	Reuse facilitation, education and support, both organisational and technical are provided.	4
3.	Individuals in the company received the necessary facilitation, education and support activities.	2
4.	A documented explicitly policy specifies the facilitation, education and support activities.	3
5.	Skilled teams of reuse facilitators, educators and support exist.	2
6.	Training programmes for reuse have been developed.	2
7.	Projects are launched with specific role for facilitators.	3
8.	Project and company education covers reuse.	2
9.	company wide support is provided for reuse.	1
10.	Measurements of training and support offered, per customer are available.	1
11.	The role of the facilitators and support staff are reviewed with the project managers.	2

Figure 2- Example of a KRA assessment

A low score in any key activity highlights areas which need immediate attention and improvement.

Summary

There are two sets of requisites in any reuse programme. First is dictated by *business* goals and objectives, second is the requirements of the reuse process itself. This is manifested in Reuse Maturity Models.

Each approach can be employed separately. However, a holistic measurement programme must address both needs. Employing the GQM without the RMM approach may prove inadequate because the required infrastructure to adhere to reuse is not in place.

The GQM paradigm is adapted for reuse by incorporating multi-views of the reuse participants in the paradigm. This is demonstrated in the paper through a case study.

RMM is taken a step further. It is no longer merely offering a framework for institutionalising reuse. It is used actively for self assessment and continual stepwise process improvements.

In our approach GQM and RMM point to products, processes and resources which require improvement. Figure 1 indicates that planning and co-ordinating these improvements can be performed centrally to achieve coherent results.

References

1. Barnes, BAH., Bollinger, T.B., "Making Reuse Cost-Effective", IEEE Software, January 1991.

2. Basili, V.R., Rombach, H.D., "The Tame Project: Towards Improvement-Oriented Software Environments", IEEE Transactions on Software Engineering, 14(6), 1988, pp 758-773.

3. Daskalantonakis, M.K., "Achieving Higher SEI Levels", IEEE Software, July 1994.

4. Fenton, N.E., "Software Metrics: A Rigorous Approach", Chapman & Hall, 1991.

5. Griss, M.L., Latour, L., editors, Proceedings of WISR'92, the 5th Annual Workshop on Institutionalising Software Reuse, Computer Science Department, University of Maine, October 1992.

6. Prieto-Diaz, R., Freeman, P., "Classifying Software for Reusability", IEEE Software, January 1987.

7. Sarshar, M., "Software Reuse and Reusability Metrics", in Object Orientation, Unicom Publications, Uxbridge, 1995.

Appendix A

A sample evaluation sheet for assessing KRAs.

	Approach	Deployment	Results
1	• No management recognition of need. • No organisational ability or commitment.	• No part of the organisation uses the practice.	• Ineffective.
2	• Management has begun to recognise the need. • Support items for the practice start to be created. • A few parts of organisation are able to implement the practice.	• Fragmented use. • Inconsistent use. • Deployed in some part of the organisation. • Limited monitoring /verification of use.	• Spotty result. • Inconsistent results • some evidence of effectiveness for some parts of the organisation.
3	• Wide but not complete commitment by management. • Road map for practice implementation defined. • Several supporting items for the practice in place.	• Some consistency in use. • Deployed in some major parts of the organisation. • Verification of use for several parts of the organisation.	• Consistent and positive results for several parts of the organisation. • Inconsistent results • for other parts of the organisation.
4	• Management commitment. • Practice implement well under way across parts of the organisation, as an integral part of most processes. • Supporting items encourage and facilitate the use of the practice.	• Consistency use across parts of the organisation. • Deployed in almost all parts of the organisation. • Monitoring /verification of use for parts of the organisation.	• Positive measurable results in almost all parts of the organisation. • Consistently positive results over time across almost all parts of the organisation.
5	• Management provides zealous leadership and commitment. • Organisational excellence in the practice recognised even outside the company.	• Consistency use over time across all parts of the organisation. • Verification for all parts of the organisation.	• Requirements exceeded. • Consistently world-class results. • Counsel sought by others.

(1) = poor; (2) = weak; (3) = fair; (4) = good; (5) = excellent.

Technology Issues of Software Reuse

Chas W Church PhD
Advanced Software Centre, Hitachi Europe Limited
Maidenhead, United Kingdom

Abstract

There is adequate available technology for the software reuse process and the real organisational impediment is the lack of managerial and developer commitment. This may be overcome with tools which facilitate low-commitment entry programmes and the incremental improvement of the reusable resource.

KEYWORDS: software development, software libraries, software reuse, software tools, legacy code, subversive reuse.

1 Introduction

It would be very comforting to report that the widespread adoption of software reuse was awaiting the development and introduction of appropriate technology. Yes, we all know that software reuse is a *good thing* but, sorry, the tools are not yet available so we shall just have to muddle through in the same old way. Maybe in the future, when the technology is in place. But, for now, let's cut some code.

However, the excuses are no good. Although technological progress will continue to make the process easier, software reuse is not radically impeded by the lack of tools and technology. Most of the technology is already in place and is entirely adequate for supporting effective software reuse. The real impediment is the individual software developer, his management and the *"reuse-unfriendly"* nature of most software development environments.

In order to justify such a view we must first take a fairly basic look at software reuse. Software reuse is about finding some existing code that, to a greater or lesser extent, performs the function that you need for your current application and incorporating it, as it is or adapted in some way, into that current application. Of course, the theoreticians will endlessly argue about issues such as the rights and wrongs of adapting code or reusing it in its original pristine, maintainable state. And the enthusiastic abstractricians amongst us will look towards Heaven and tell us about reusing designs, design patterns and even dreams. However, taking a pragmatic view, ignoring the academic niceties and deferring Heaven for the mid-future, the basic idea of software reuse is as just stated. It is about finding and profitably reusing existing code. And, for reuse to be possible, there has to be some sort of code asset to be reused. Such code assets may exist in several forms, such as third-party reusable libraries, internal reusable libraries developed by a particular organisation, developers' personal libraries or, as will often be the case in the early days of a reuse programme, existing applications known or thought to contain "useful" code. Such existing applications probably come within the definition of "legacy code" although this term seems somehow to imply monumental edifices of mainframe code of dubious value. In our definition "existing applications" are comparatively recent or may even be concurrent projects to that for which reuse is being considered.

2 Reuse Process and Roles

Let us examine the reuse process in a little more detail to determine the "tools and technology" needed by those participating in it. And, to begin with, let us see who is involved in the process. Within Hitachi we tend to talk of the "Developer", the "User" and the "Administrator". This terminology is fairly arbitrary but is a useful shorthand for describing a series of roles which, quite often, are overlapping and undertaken by the same individual on different occasions during his work. So, solely, for convenience, we shall use these terms from now on.

The Developer is really the first link in the reuse chain. But he/she does not undertake any actual reuse. His/her job is to develop the code (which we have termed "internal reusable libraries" above) to be later reused within the same organisation by the "User". Of course, developers of commercial third-party libraries are also "Developers" within our terminology but, for the present, we shall just consider the in-house Developer.

So Developers develop reusable code. Tough job for clever people. And who can tell if they have succeeded in developing anything reusable until someone reuses it? However, setting aside such issues, what is the difference in developing reusable code to any other code? In terms of the development environment, nothing. It is just the same old editors, debuggers and such like. Of course, somebody smart may eventually come along who will offer a tool to measure/critique/assist the "reusability" of code. Presumably if a knowledgeable developer can design something reusable and check when he has done it then such knowledge can be incorporated into some form of Reuse Assistant. However, until and if such gadget comes along, the Developer has all that he needs to develop reusable code. So there is no impeding lack of "tools and technology" in the "Developers" area.

We have already mentioned the "User" so let us visit him/her next. The User is just the application developer who either desires or, more likely, has been managerially enthused, to undertake as much code reuse as possible in developing his/her applications. Another tough job. But not everybody can be clever. The User is surrounded by masses of so-called reusable code but has no idea what, if anything, is suitable for the current task. Worse still, even if something reusable exists, the User has no idea where it is in the mass of third-party and internal reusable libraries or, worst of all, heaps of existing *un-reuse-structured* existing applications. It is a sort of Needle-in-the-Haystack problem with the additional complication that the search is actually for a drawing pin.

So is this the Achilles Heel of software reuse? Is this where it all becomes impossible? No - because this is the one area where specific reuse technology is both needed and actually exists. Hitachi's ObjectReuser is just one of several products which address the problem of rapidly assisting the User to find appropriate code for the needs of their current application. Such products, working either at the "information" or "source code" level, or both, enable the User to make the best match between their requirements and the available resource. But because reuse of code is largely dependent on the quality of information about it this process can be very easily confounded by lack of discipline at the "Developer" stage. Or by lack of User commitment. Nevertheless, it is not a problem of the lack of "tools and technology". If code is in a reasonably reusable form, it can be quickly accessed and reused. If the code is not in a form suitable for reuse then the problem gets harder or, maybe, impossible.

There may often be a third actor in the process. This we call the “Administrator” or “Librarian”. In many organisations this role will be taken on by one of the Developers or, in a more laissez-faire style of working, may not exist at all. The Administrator is the custodian of an organisation’s repository of reusable code, whether or not this is bought in from third-party library vendors or is the result of in-house effort. In some organisations where reuse is well-established the Administrator will be responsible for imposing fairly strict control over the content of the repository so that, for instance, although Developers may access reusable code in all stages of development status, Users may only access reusable code that has been properly Quality Assured. Thus, in such a system of working, the Administrator is very much responsible for Lifecycle Management of reusable assets.

So how about tools for the Administrator? Are there sufficient tools for him/her to discipline the reuse process, if that is what an organisation wants? Again, no problem. In fact there is a surfeit of solutions. For a dedicated reuse-specific solution there is ObjectReuser’s LifeCycle Management facility which will enable the Administrator to very fully monitor and control the development and use of reusable code. But, more generally, it must again be asked what is the special characteristic of reusable code that sets it apart from any other code developed and used within an organisation? The answer is simple when it is realised that, although the Administrator will adhere to reuse-specific principles, his basic tools are those for configuration management, version control and access management. And, if an organisation is sufficiently *reuse-advanced* to require the proper administration of its reusable code assets then, presumably, it will already have some effective configuration management and version control tools to discipline its day-to-day application code development. So, maybe the Administrator will need to be trained to support a proper corporate reuse philosophy.

However, it is very unlikely that he will lack the existing tools to support that philosophy.

Developer, User and Administrator. We have reasonably covered all the roles in the reuse process and, although not all the tools may have *"Reuse Compatible"* on the box, there does not seem to be a fundamental lack of reuse technology. If an organisation and the individuals within it are committed to reuse then there is a sufficient armoury of tools, many of which may already be in place, for all of the actors to play their roles very adequately. But then few organisations or individuals are committed to reuse. So having disposed of the great *"tools excuse"* let us turn to the real reuse inhibitor, the lack of organisational and personal commitment. And then, maybe, we will come back to tools again.

3 Commitment

In this time of short-term economics it would be a brave senior IT manager who committed his organisation to a major reuse programme. A little pilot project dabbling will escape the notice of the corporate bean counters but the person responsible for a serious reuse programme is an obvious candidate for the Job Club. Because reuse can be expensive, the benefits are not be immediately obvious and the clever people who know how to write reusable code will demand ludicrous salaries. So the shortage of organisational commitment is rather understandable.

And how about individuals? Software development is the last bastion to defy the Industrial Revolution. Why should the codesman's skills be sacrificed on the altar of mass production? Why should the same boring old components be used over and over again as a denial of the creativity of the individual *software artiste*? Why grope around for reusable code when there is a clean fresh screen on which to write your own bug-ridden masterpiece? So maybe the words are an exaggeration. But we all know that there is much more than an ounce of truth in them.

So tools were not the problem. But organisational and individual commitment to reuse is the key impediment. And it is wholly understandable. Reuse can endanger your job if you are a manager and can seriously threaten your fun if you are a programmer.

4 Subversive Reuse Tools

Is there an answer to the "commitment" issue that we have so painfully proven to be the root cause of our problems? Yes, and we turn full circle to return to reuse tools. And, to be specific, *subversive* reuse tools.

Except in the boldest and richest organisations it seems that a full-frontal approach to reuse cannot easily succeed. But, although investment in reuse cannot be immediately recovered, the mid-to-long term savings and increases in productivity, quality and maintainability are very considerable. Therefore the responsible and aware IT manager will endorse reuse introduction providing it can be accomplished substantially risk-free. Thus reuse must enter quietly, cheaply and should not attract the attention of the nice accountants who rightfully run the organisation. And it is in the nature of the tools that this trick can be accomplished.

Hopefully we have already established the basic adequacy of the available tools. Now we must turn to their ability to support the subversive introduction of reuse into organisations. And what do we mean by "*subversive*"? Essentially it refers the fuss-free but effective introduction of reuse into an organisation that is not culturally *"reuse-friendly"*. Again, we will look at the essentials of the process before discussing the needs and adequacies of the tools.

A properly funded reuse programme demands that properly designed and documented reusable assets are available *up front* in advance of the widescale adoption of reuse practices by application developers. In essence, reuse cannot begin to take place unless there is some reasonably ship-shape code to reuse. And a software disciplinarian needs to be hired to ensure that the hackers do not adaptively mutate the assets into all possible directions. But such luxuries cannot be guaranteed in a *subversive* or *soft-entry* reuse programme. Probably the best assets to be expected are some variously documented third-party and corporate libraries plus the ubiquitous mass of existing application code. So the need is for tools that can effectively scavenge and convert such resources into a half-decent organised, documented and relatively user-friendly resource for application developers. And beyond this, the need is for further tools which will actively support and encourage recalcitrant application developers to explore such a contrived reuse resource, albeit with its inevitable shortcomings, and both productively use its content for currently-developed applications and, in parallel, incrementally strengthen the resource for future users. And finally, hovering in the shadows, there must be a ruthless but unwaged configuration management android to maintain the integrity of the reusable resource.

It is not appropriate to explain such concepts in terms of a particular commercial software development tool. However, an analogy might be useful. Let us suppose the removal men manage to completely randomise our collection of books when we move house. Our once organised library is a complete shambles on the floor of our new home. We do not have the time or inclination to properly reorganise our books but bribe and cajole our children to help us roughly categorise the volumes as they place them on their new shelves. The end result is fairly chaotic but, at least, the sheet music is separated from the dictionaries and the tomes on software engineering are reasonably distinct from the gardening books. We can close the door with a sigh and join in the hunt for the cat.

Life returns to normal and we slowly start to reuse our library. Of course, it is not so easy as before but the rough categorisation made by the kids is sufficient to enable us to find the books that we need. And, once we have consulted a particular volume, we can insert it back in its "proper" position and either remember or label the shelf accordingly. So, over time, our library once again becomes well-organised and pleasurable to use. And we didn't need to purchase any replacement books or devote immense "start-up" time to reorganising everything.

It is not a very good analogy but the ideas should be obvious, especially in respect of incremental improvement of library organisation and quality of documentation. Tools which do the "kid's work" of initial categorisation automatically and then assist in the incremental access and categorisation improvement with usage over time are already available and ably facilitate the *subversive* or *soft-entry* form of reuse programmes outlined above. And since it is the entry stage of an effective reuse programme which is the main stumbling block to effective long-term reuse then it is such tools which hold the key to success in establishing effective corporate software reuse programmes.

5 Summary

Our summary is short and simple. There is already enough technology on the table for effective reuse programmes to be mounted. But managerial and developer commitment is lacking. And the reasons are understandable. So the tools have to go one step further and must both pre-process the initial reusable resources, which are likely to be unattractive, poorly documented and uncategorised, and must then offer developers a route to find and reuse the resources and, hopefully, leave them in a little better state than when he/she found them.

Finding Reusable Components: by Good Luck or Good Management?

Roger A Chambers
NatWest Group IT
London, UK

Abstract

This paper proposes that different kinds of reusable components involve different levels of cost savings, and different mixes of responsibilities for component users and component suppliers. As the expected level of savings increases, so the balance of these responsibilities shifts from being user-focused to being supplier-focused. The latter involves new patterns of investment and support costs which are only likely to be accepted as part of a strategic initiative for managing the software asset base. Unless all these factors are carefully matched and managed, then reuse goals may prove elusive.

Keywords: software reuse, software components, object-orientation, conceptual model

1 Introduction

There is to my knowledge no "magic formula" that is guaranteed to grant success to an organisation seeking to define which objects it should try to acquire and promote as reusable components. We cannot formulate simple answers because the nature of a "reusable component" will vary considerably between organisations, or even within an organisation, as the approach to systems development evolves. Thus the best we can do in considering this topic is to look at the underlying issues which can affect our choice of strategies for component selection and reuse.

First I believe it is vital to be clear over what it is we are trying to reuse and why, i.e. what are the components and what benefits does their reuse confer? Further, if we are able to define components but not acquire them, or acquire components but not use them to build our systems then they are obviously not reusable. Thus we must address the issue of the skills and resources we have or need to support reuse, if we are to be able to define components which are reusable in our own development environments. Also, since reuse involves some degree of investment we must consider how well our reuse initiative fits within our broader systems development aims and strategies. Only when we set reuse in this broader context can we start to recognise how to define the components we should be seeking to acquire (definition for supply) and how to help our developers identify the components they should reuse (definition for demand).

2 Reusable Components

2.1 Types of Reusable Components

A commonly encountered view is that reuse, particularly in an OO environment, is primarily concerned with sharing pre-coded classes from a class library, e.g. the native classes in SmallTalk or the Microsoft Foundation Classes for C++. However the spectrum of potential reuse is actually much wider. For the purposes of this paper I will use the following categories:

- Analysis and Design (A&D) Models - these models capture knowledge about the "business" (a term I shall use here for any target environment in which we are implementing systems) and the way in which it does, should, or could work. If the business has not changed significantly since a model was built then it should be possible to reuse it, or parts of it, rather than starting again from scratch. Most business models are built in-house but an external market is emerging for some forms of domain-specific models, e.g. for banking, insurance, etc.

- Source Code (OO classes) - this is a well recognised form of reusable component, traceable back to subroutine libraries, that can be built in-house or purchased. Initially the purchased components have been smaller, more technical items, e.g. for building GUI's, but recently libraries of larger, more inter-related classes have become available, e.g. a library of C++ classes for rules definition and inference to support the development of knowledge-based systems (KBS).

- Executables - these components are supplied in a form which can be embedded, linked, or otherwise invoked in an application, but not amended, e.g. a pre-compiled unit of software, an OLE object, etc. Usually such components are supplied empty of business data content which is added as part of their installation or use. This is typically the form in which moderate to large units of third-party software are purchased but it can be used for components developed in-house.

- Subsystems - these are usually larger, more complex components which can be invoked through a specific interface, usually as servers in a client / server architecture. Typically subsystems are unique within an enterprise (unless deliberately partitioned or duplicated, e.g. for performance reasons) and are the sole source of a particular type of information or service. They are usually implemented and run in-house, though they may be assembled from components in the previous categories. However a few subsystems can be licensed from external suppliers for remote invocation, e.g. stock exchange data feeds.

Having recognised this variation in the type of reusable components we can use it as a basis for analysing variations in the range of benefits offered by the reuse of each type of component, which in commercial terms usually reduces to potential cost savings.

2.2 Development & Support Savings

In analysing the potential savings in reusing a component we need to review the full range of costs across a system's life cycle. Using experience and common sense, rather than hard data which is very difficult to obtain, I have roughly estimated the level of possible savings to be gained from reusing the four categories of components described above (ignoring for the time being the cost of achieving the reuse). I have done this under the following categories of development and support effort:

- Analysis & Design (A & D)
    - Reusing any of the three types of coded components, i.e. Source Code, Executables, or Subsystems, implies an acceptance of the underlying analysis and design and thus a good potential for savings in A & D effort.
    - Reusing A & D models which are not accompanied with an implementation may save repeating similar effort but will often involve additional effort to fit the designs to a particular implementation platform. In most of the remaining categories of effort this type of reuse involves no savings and so it will only be mentioned again if there is some potential gain.
- Coding
    - Reusing Subsystems or Executables, with no access to the code, obviously saves the effort to produce that code.
    - Reusing Source Code in a disciplined way also saves coding effort but it is often difficult to maintain discipline and prevent uncontrolled, uncoordinated modifications which lead to component proliferation and reduction or loss of the savings. Also, heavily modified code is often more costly and error-prone than components designed and coded from scratch.
- Unit Testing - but not systems testing[1].
    - Assuming adequate quality is delivered by the supplier, reuse of Subsystems or Executables should involve minimal unit testing.
    - Reusing Source Code will involve some effort here. Even if the original code is of impeccable quality there is always a risk of

[1] System testing focuses on how all the components work together as a whole, and since new systems will usually involve new combinations, the use or reuse of different component types is not likely to affect system testing significantly.

transcription errors, compiler incompatibilities, etc., and even "simple" changes risk compromising the integrity of the whole component.

- Data Management - this is taken to include the establishment and management of the databases or files necessary to support the component, including any data entry, conversions, bridges, etc.
    - Since Subsystems are assumed to have the necessary data management support in place, reuse has good potential savings.
    - Both Executables and source Code may provide support in this area, and possibly more with executables, but some additional effort is typically required for each reuse.

    Reusing A & D models may simplify data management by encouraging common data standards and simplifying data sharing and data exchange interfaces.

- Implementation (including acceptance)
    - As a Subsystem which is being reused will already have been implemented and should have well understood user characteristics it should give good savings in this area.
    - A reused executable will still need some implementation effort and its performance in the new context may be less predictable.
    - Reused Source Code, particularly if modified, may not save much effort here.

- Maintenance
    - For reused Subsystems and Executables all changes, whether error corrections or enhancements, have to be channelled through the component supplier and will be carried out on the master version of the component. This allows, or even forces, "batching" of changes and sharing of testing effort. The cost of the maintenance is also shared across multiple users so the potential for savings is good.
    - Reused Source Code may be maintained centrally but this is difficult to enforce as it is usually very easy to make changes locally. As a result maintenance effort tends to be dispersed and often duplicated, so savings in this area may be limited.

- Supporting Further Reuse - as will be seen later, supporting reuse requires effort. Under this category I estimate the extent to which the effort spent in supporting one reuse of a component will save effort in supporting subsequent reuse.
    - Successful reuse of a Subsystem component, with its high potential for savings in development effort for the reusers, can build a "bandwagon"

effect which facilitates the "selling" of subsequent reuse, though some support effort will always be required.

- Successful reuse of Executables, Source Code, or A & D Models can also encourage others into reuse, but as the potential savings to the reusers decreases so the need for continuing reuse support increases.

The estimated savings described above are shown below in tabular form with the level of saving classed as Low (L), Medium (M), or High (H).

Component Category	Analysis & Design Saving	Coding Saving	Unit Test Saving	Data Management Saving	Implementation Saving	Maintenance Saving	Further Reuse Support Saving
Sub-system	H	H	H	H	M-H	M	M
Executable	H	H	H	M-H	M	M	L-M
Source code	H	M-H	M	M	L	L	L-M
A&D model	M-H	-	-	L	-	-	L

Table 1. Potential Savings by Component Category

The inferences that can be drawn from this table will be considered later in conjunction with the analysis of the support implications for the different component categories.

2.3 Component Support Implications

We can uncover some further implications of component reuse if we look at the activities involved in reusing components from our four categories, and analyse how the division of responsibility for them varies between the component supplier and the component user, i.e. the application builders. We will view the responsibilities as referring to the implemented application component. This will be either the reused component itself, a copy of it, or a further development based on it depending on the category of reuse involved.

The analysis is presented in the table below. The first column shows an activity not considered in the previous section. It relates to the publishing of the reusable component and includes change management and version control. The next four columns refer to activities described earlier, or combinations of them. The last two columns separate out the responsibilities for implementing the component itself from those of integrating it with the other components to form the full application system. In the table the responsibilities of the supplier are represented as S, and those of the user as U.

Component Category	Publish Component Version	Analysis & Design	Coding & Unit Test	Maintenance	Data Management	Implement Component	System Integration
Sub-system	S	S	S	S	S	S	U
Executable	S	S	S	S	U/S	U	U
Source Code	S	S	S/U	U/S	U	U	U
A&D Model	S	S/U	U	U	U	U	U

Table 2. Component Responsibilities by Component Category

Comparing this table with the previous one it becomes obvious that as we progress from reuse of A & D models up to the reuse of subsystems, the scope of potential savings increases considerably but this is accompanied by a shift in development and support responsibilities from the component user to the component supplier. This raises a very important point, namely that no matter how good we are at identifying and defining components with a high potential for reuse, if our development organisations are not geared up to provide the required levels of supporting effort and skills then reuse will not occur. To examine this further let us look in outline at the development process.

3 The Development Process

3.1 The "Craft Shop" Approach

The traditional "craft shop" approach to IT development is one in which each "product" (model, system, etc.) is built from scratch in response to a unique set of requirements and developed independently, as shown in the figure below.

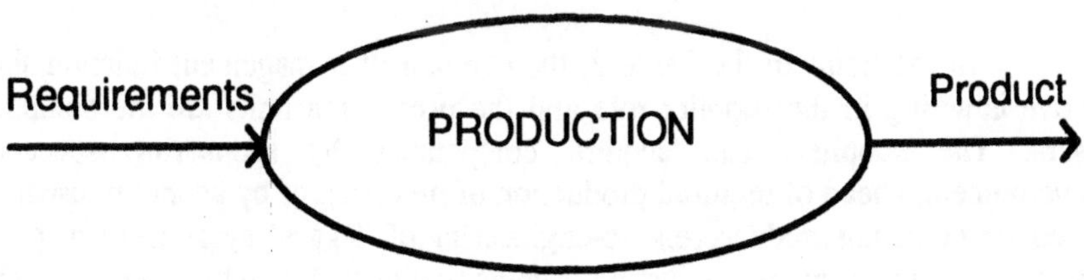

Figure 1. Production under the "Craft Shop" Approach

Some degree of inter-project co-ordination can be achieved through strategic planning and systems architectures but these often control only the overall scope and external interfaces of the larger products, such as major systems, and their influence is limited by the independence which development projects have usually enjoyed. Under this approach all the development effort is focused on current production with little, if any, directed towards component management and support. In organisations based on this pattern, reuse across projects is highly unlikely and even within projects is likely to be constrained to reuse of simple model or source code components.

3.2 The "Factory" Approach

In the "factory" approach to development some requirements can be met by reusable components, including designs as well as finished units of software. Co-ordination can then be achieved by acquiring and managing components which meet requirements which are common across projects, including those which support or enforce required standards. Being common, the components must be managed separately for the common good as shown in the diagram below.

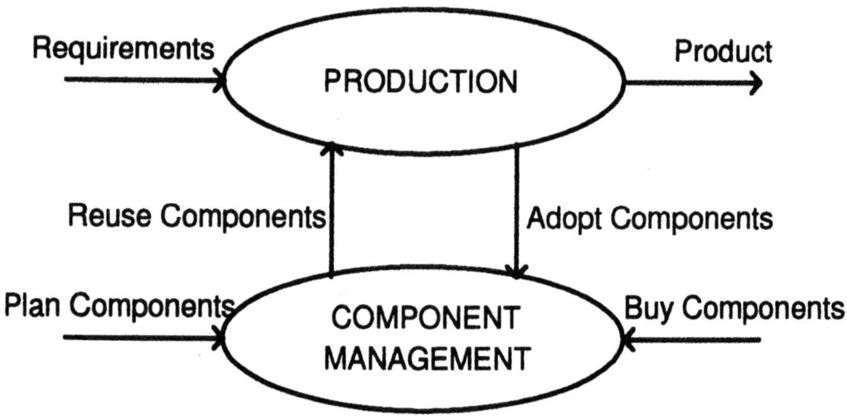

Figure 2. Production under the "Factory" Approach

In the terms of the Table 2, the component management function shown above is acting in the supplier role and the production units are the component users. The suppliers can acquire components by sponsoring speculative development, ahead of required production of products, or by adoption, usually by reworking existing products (e.g. re-engineering of "legacy" systems) or by putting extra effort into on-going production. Acquisition may also be by external purchase but though this is increasingly possible for technical OO components, markets for business object components are still being developed.

Adopting this kind of development approach obviously opens the opportunity for more systematic reuse of components, but again, the implications of Table 2 are that we must put enough of the right kind of skills and effort into component management to match the level of component we are trying to reuse. This forces us to consider our reuse initiatives in a wider, strategic context.

4 Component Migration Strategy

4.1 Component Levels and Numbers

A recent Gartner Group Research Note [1] looked at migration strategies for making the transition from large, monolithic systems to application composed of finer-grained software units, typically objects. It presented the problem in a helpful diagram, reproduced below, which allows companies to contrast the approximate average size and number of their current software units with the size and number of units in their desired target state.

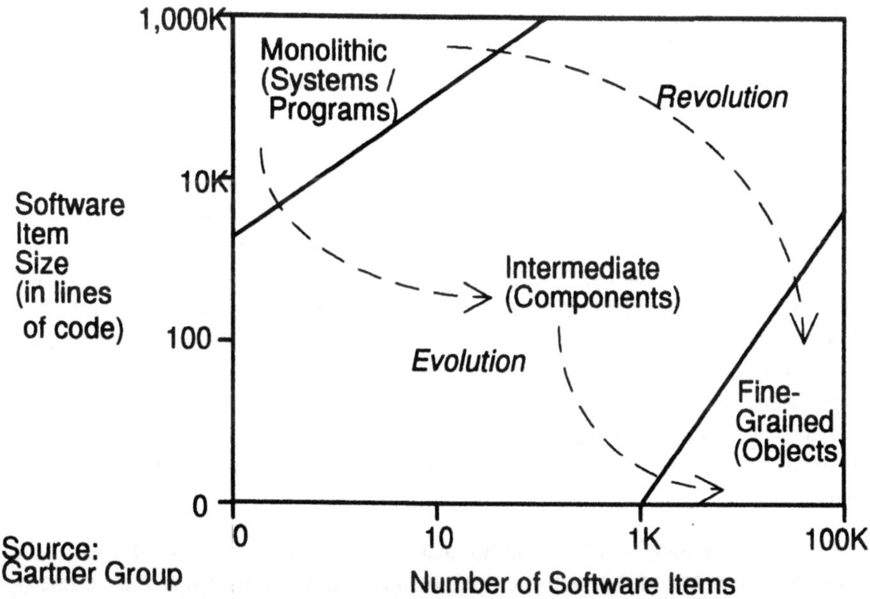

Figure 3. Component Migration of Software Inventory

Seen in this context it becomes obvious that attempting to make the transition directly to objects is a revolutionary strategy in which there is a wholesale replacement of the older systems with the new ones. The category of components most likely to be reused in such circumstances is Source Code, e.g. class libraries.

Many companies with a large and costly systems inventory cannot afford such a radical change. They can only justify the transition if it proceeds via a more gradual, evolutionary strategy. This would seek to reuse parts of the older systems, separating them out as reusable components made available as executables or as encapsulated subsystems, possibly using object "wrappers". This approach does not necessarily involve the use of OO technology. As long as the supporting technical architecture provides some form of "middleware" to allow components to invoke each other, they can be implemented in any technology which supports an interface to the middleware. Later these components, shown as "Intermediate" in fig. 3, can be split into even finer-grained items by re-engineering or replacing them, typically when there is a business need to extend or change their functionality. This is a point where the introduction of OO technology could be considered, possibly even on a component-by-component basis. Work at this stage should be much more manageable, in any implementation technology, as the intermediate components are already much smaller than the original systems from which they were taken.

4.2 Reacting to Component Demand

If either of the two component migration strategies is attempted in an organisation with a predominantly "craft shop" development approach then the need to identify and define reusable components will be largely driven by the demands of individual projects. This is dangerous because even if a project recognises the wider reuse potential of a component that it could build or adapt as an executable or a subsystem, it will probably lack the time and resources to produce it in a fully reusable form, and there will be no component management infrastructure to provide support services for it. Thus reuse is likely to be confined to the "less profitable" category of Source Code which requires less support. Also without the necessary promotion and management of reuse, even the components that are produced may not be accepted outside the originating project, and similar components may proliferate across projects. Indeed there is much anecdotal evidence that even companies making significant investments in OO development are experiencing the growth of multiple "islands" of similar but incompatible objects.

If a "factory" approach is adopted then the resources and infrastructure will be put in place to manage the components and coordinate the reuse strategy. While being better able to support reuse of the more sophisticated Executable and Subsystem components, this approach can still allow longer-term corporate requirements to be overridden by immediate project requirements, with the attendant risks of lack of generality and eventual proliferation of the components. The factory approach also faces its own risks connected with the extent of the cultural change and the size of the investment needed to make it work.

4.3 Coordinating Component Supply

If the risks outlined above are to be avoided it is necessary to implement the factory approach with component supply and management being done in a more proactive way, anticipating and coordinating demand rather than just reacting to it. To see what may be involved in this we can take the previous diagram one stage further. First we can see, in terms of a company's total systems inventory, that the upper right of the diagram represents the undesirable situation of having too many components for a given average size, while the lower left area represents the impractical situation of having too few component of too small a size. Within the remaining area we can look for ways of balancing size and number of components to improve manageability of the software asset base and maximise the likelihood of reuse.

One means of doing this is to modify our end goal from one seeking to assemble applications directly from fine-grained components to one which encourages reuse at the level of coarser-grained components, e.g. object clusters. These will typically be supplied for reuse as executables or subsystems, but may be composed internally of the finer-grained components to give them a modular structure which the component suppliers can easily adapt to meet changes in requirements from new or existing component users. The additional concepts are show in fig. 4 in a revised version of the previous diagram.

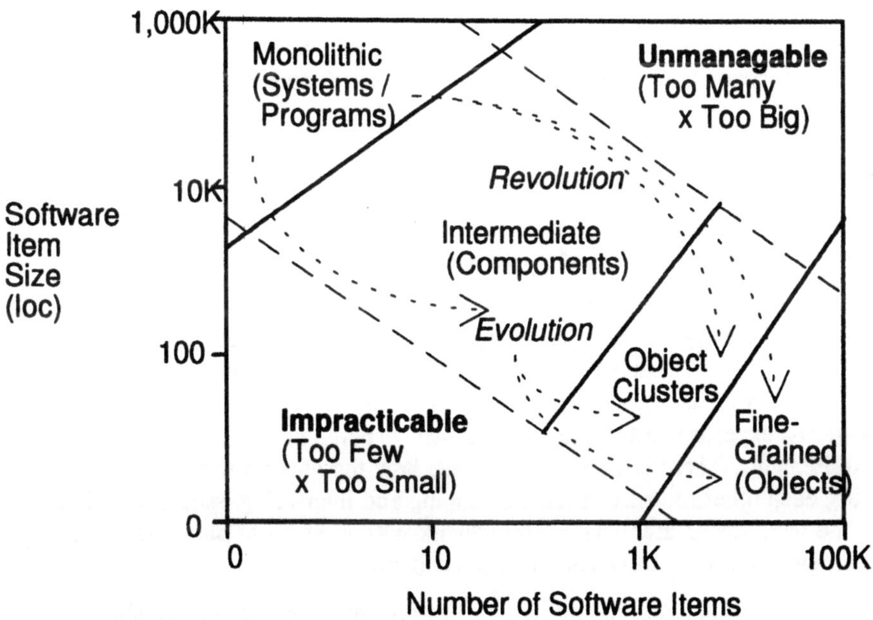

Figure 4. Component Migration - Balancing Size and Number

4.4 Granularity & Control

With typical applications often containing hundreds of classes, it has been recognised for some time that there is a need for some kind of system building block larger than an object or class in order to reduce complexity and make systems more understandable and more manageable. In the context of reuse, the diagram illustrates how seeking reuse at the level of clusters reduces the number of published components. Since most languages do not support clustering, many methodologists have introduced design concepts and notations to reflect this kind of structure. Unfortunately, other than agreeing on the need, there is little in common between their proposals and even the choice of names differs widely, including assembly, class category, cluster, domain, high-level object class, kit, module, pattern, subject, and subsystem. Firesmith [2] surveys current proposals and outlines a way of drawing together some of the common strands, but as yet there is little evidence of consensus or of support for this kind of structure in languages or CASE tools.

The lack of support from methods and languages makes it hard to publish clusters as Source Code, so they are more likely to be offered as Executables or Subsystems. For such components there are a variety of technical infrastructure components, either available or being developed, to provide practical ways of invoking or embedding them in application systems, e.g. Microsoft's OLE for Executables or various forms of remote procedure call (RPC) for Subsystems.

Working at this higher level of granularity also makes it possible to "mix and match" an evolutionary and a revolutionary approach to component migration. If the chosen technical architecture contains a suitable "middleware" component enabling cooperation between intermediate sized components within a larger application, then it does not matter whether the components are parts of existing systems that have been reworked or "wrapped", or are specially designed and developed object clusters.

4.5 A Route Map for Migration

While it is relatively easy to suggest individual classes as candidates for reuse, particularly for technical or specialised business objects, the identification and definition of reusable object clusters requires particular skills in conceptual thinking as well as a broad view of the target business area and access to a range of business expertise, either through actual experts or their written ideas and requirements. There is also a need to see how the clusters relate to, and interact with, each other in order to resolve scoping and interfacing issues. All this points to the need for an architectural framework within which to plan and manage the strategies for both component migration and reuse.

One approach to this which has already received considerable research attention is the ARPA Domain-Specific Software Architecture (DSSA) Program which was described to the BCS Reuse Group by Will Tracz last year [3]. This approach has focused on the highly technical and specialised domain of avionics, but many of the findings and recommendations apply to the more general commercial world. In this broader field a sub-group of the OMG, the Business Object Management Special Interest Group (BOMSIG) is addressing the problems of defining and supporting ".. a cross-section or horizontal layer of business objects that ... vertical applications can use" [4]. Here the term "vertical" is being applied to specific domains such as finance, manufacturing, geographic information, etc., which may be traversed by a single business processes in a commercial organisation.

Our own experience in NatWest Group IT [5] is that a single, conceptual, OO model, in our case the Business Reference Model (BRM), is of very great value in helping us to coordinate our migration towards a component-based approach to application development.

5 The Role of a Conceptual Model in Reuse

5.1 Model Objectives and Benefits

A single, conceptual model of a domain or an enterprise establishes a common language with which the business and IT communities can describe requirements, possible solutions, and the context in which they fit, with more structure and rigour, and less ambiguity, than is common, or even possible, with plain text. Defining all components in terms of the structures of such a model encourages a high level of consistency in meaning and operation which facilitates the integration of such components into effective applications. Also since the scope of the model is usually broader than that of any individual component or application, it enables these to be seen in a wider context and facilitates the resolution of local scoping and interfacing issues.

Ideally the model should also be modular, e.g. supporting some form of object "clustering" and preferably also cluster "nesting", with tight binding within modules and loose coupling between them. If so, the modules become good candidates for implementation as software components, and applications built with such components should exhibit considerable flexibility with respect to the way in which components can be added, changed, or recombined to meet future changes in requirements.

Finally, defining components for many applications based on a single model of this nature facilitates the recognition of commonality between applications and so supports and encourages reuse. This can be by both the revolutionary route, choosing to build or acquire a totally new component to meet a set of requirements, or by the evolutionary route, mapping old systems and new requirements to the model and recognising that they have one or more of the model concepts in common, already implemented in a form that could be reworked into a reusable component.

5.2 Model-Related Processes Supporting Reuse

Building, maintaining, and using a common conceptual model requires a mandate and resources which go beyond the scope of any single application development project. Thus such an initiative cannot be attempted without putting in place at least some elements of the component management function of the "factory" approach to development. This involves new processes, not present in the "craft shop" approach, which contribute to the costs of supporting and promoting reuse, mentioned earlier in the paper.

One of the key processes in NatWest's use of our BRM model is "alignment". Here members of a central team work with IT and business staff at the earliest possible stage of a project, typically starting from the definition of outline requirements, to map the problem / requirement statement on to NatWest's published architectures, including the BRM which is our information architecture. The key deliverable from the alignment process is an issues list which can raise issues both against the project and the architectures.

Issues for the project typically concern scope (e.g. overlaps with other projects or existing systems which have already been aligned), divergence from the architectures (e.g. for the BRM, differently defined or misapplied concepts, boundary definitions which do not fit the modular structure of the model, etc.), and equivalences with the model (e.g. list of project concepts which are equivalent to some part of the BRM). The list of equivalences will typically be used to generate a list of candidate components for reuse by the project. The list will at the least will contain A & D sub-models taken from the BRM, but may also, as a follow-on from the scoping issues, include lists of code, executable, or subsystem components that the project may be able to either use as supplied, rework from existing systems, or develop as a new addition to the component asset base.

Issues against the BRM typically concern perceived deficiencies in the model. These can include a project concept being new to the model, either totally or as a new specialisation of an existing concept, and projects identifying scenarios which act as counter cases highlighting potential flaws in the model. In resolving such issues the model becomes richer and more robust, and thus an even better tool to support reuse. However the resources needed to publish and maintain the model need to be part of a central group and are yet another part of the cost of reuse that must be born or allocated in some way.

5.3 Resolving Reuse Issues

The issues raised against the architectural models can be resolved if the "factory" approach has been accepted and the relevant central resources have been provided and funded. However the issues raised against the project, including whether or not to accept recommendations on reuse and on the acquisition, by whatever means, of specific components to reuse, usually reduce to issues of cost, time, and business priority. These can usually only be resolved by the business sponsor of the application. Because robust, generic, reusable components take more time and effort to produce than single-purpose, one-off components, there will be times when the longer-term interests of reuse will be overridden by shorter-term business priorities, particularly when the available stock of reusable components is small and many with good potential for reuse still need to be acquired. Even in these circumstances alignment to an architectural model has benefits since by raising and documenting the issue it ensures that the decision not to invest in reuse is taken consciously rather than through ignorance or oversight. Also it facilitates the assessment of the impact of the decision, e.g. in terms of possible overlaps and duplication of components, and of the possibility of either moving back to the path of reuse later or of reaching some compromise, e.g. building a one-off component as a prototype of a later, reusable version.

6 Conclusions

6.1 Other Issues

The success of a reuse initiative is dependent on more factors than those discussed here. I have tried to focus on the issues which I perceive to have most impact on the way we identify and define objects for successful reuse, but even if we resolve these problems carefully, further issues such as the technology (of our Case, library, and language tools for development and support, and of our operational environment, middleware, etc.), the human factors (of skills, motivation, and culture) and the economics of reuse in our organisation, will all constrain the options open to us and the degree of our success.

6.2 Summing Up

I hope this paper serves to stimulate debate within, and possibly between companies, about the nature and aims of their software reuse strategy and whether there is a good enough match between their aspirations for reuse, their wider strategies for managing their software portfolio, and the realities of their application development organisation, both in terms of its structure and resources, and its role in the internal and / or external market for software products. While much of what has been presented here is based on our experience in NatWest Group IT and has particular relevance to an approach using OO technology, the need for a component-based approach in the context of an overall application development strategy is relevant to any attempt to achieve systematic reuse whatever the implementation technology.

Without planning and coordination of approach, even heavy investment in training, tools, libraries, browsers, etc. is unlikely to yield high levels of reuse. If a managed approach is to be followed to achieve systematic reuse, then the ideal is to maintain a minimal set of powerful, generic components meeting a wide range of common requirements - having too many similar components dilutes the reuse savings but having too few components limits reuse opportunities. Keeping such a set relevant and up-to-date involves many comparisons of different requirements and competing candidate components. I believe that to do this successfully requires the use of some form of architectural model, since without a reference framework true comparison of different objects is impossible.

References

1. Jones, N. Back to the Future - the Road from Lagacy to Objects. Gartner Group Application Development & Management Strategies 1995; (May 17) Research Note SPA-700-1167.

2. Firesmith, D.G. Clusters of Classes: A Bigger Building Block. Report on Object Analysis and Design 1994; (November-December):18-21.

3. Tracz, W. Collected Overview Reports from the DSSA Project. US Public Domain Information, via Loral Federal Systems - Owego, USA.

4. Stone, C. What's the Fuss over Business Objects? First Class (Magazine of OMG) 1995 (Spring): 2.

5. Chambers, R.A. OO Experience in a Large Enterprise. Guide Share Europe (GSE) Spring Conference - Maastricht 1995 (Proceedings to be published by GSE).

Object Technology Standards - an OMG Progress Report

Eric Leach, is the principal of Eric Leach Marketing (ELM) Ltd
ELM represents the interests of OMG in the UK.

Abstract

For the full benefits of object technology to be realised, there must be one set of object technology standards. One set of standards is something that has not been achieved before in the computer industry.

The OMG has made remarkable progress in a relatively short period of time in gaining wide consensus in the formulation of object technology standards. Without denying in any way the work of other IT standards groups, in the object technology domain the OMG's achievements and work in progress are of great significance worldwide, and hence are the subject of this paper.

Object Management Group

In May 1989, eight companies founded an organisation dedicated to fostering the development and growth of object-oriented software development. These companies were 3Com Corporation, American Airlines, Canon, Inc., Data General, Hewlett-Packard, Philips Telecommunications N.V., Sun Microsystems and Unisys Corporation. The organisation they formed is The Object Management Group (OMG). OMG is the prime driving force in the world of object technology and is an international organisation supported by over 520 information system vendors, software developers, consultants, academics, and users. The organisation's charter includes the establishment of industry guidelines and object management specifications to provide a common framework for application development. Conformance to these specifications will make it possible to develop a heterogeneous applications environment across all major hardware platforms and operating systems.

The OMG defines object management as software development that models the real world through the representation of "objects". These objects are the encapsulation of the attributes, relationships and methods of software identifiable program components. A key benefit of an object-oriented system is its ability to expand in functionality by extending existing components and adding new objects to the system. Object management results in faster application development, easier maintenance and reusable software.

The acceptance and use of object technology is widespread and growing. Virtually every major provider and user of computer systems in the world today is currently using, or planning to implement, object-oriented tools and applications. Seventeen of the world's top twenty software developers are OMG members. Of the world's top 20 IT suppliers only Compaq is not an OMG member.

1. OMG's Standards Agenda

The objectives of the OMG are to foster the technology's growth and influence its direction in the following five areas:

- Overall Architecture, Reference Model and Terms
  Industry-wide consensus on an Object Management Architecture (OMA) which includes the definition of terms and a common model for objects and their attributes, relationships and methods.

- The Object Request Broker ("CORBA")
  A communications mechanism that enables objects to send and receive messages.

- CORBAservices
  A collection of services with object interfaces that provide basic functions for realising and maintaining objects.

- CORBAfacilities
  A collection of classes and objects that provide general purpose capabilities useful to many applications.

- Application Objects
  Software components specific to particular end user applications.

OMG upgraded and reissued its Object Management Architecture Guide (OMA) [1] in 1992. This guide contains OMG's Reference Model which is the central design guideline OMG uses for the creation of a distributed object computing environment. OMG's Reference Model is a conceptual roadmap to be followed to achieve OMG's technical standards' goals. It details an internetworking set of Classes and Instances that interact: common facilities and applications that use an object request broker to access and utilise object services. The Reference Model has four main components - Object Request Broker (CORBA), Object Services (CORBAservices), Common Facilities (CORBAfacilities) and Application Objects.

One of the key components of the OMA is the OMG Object Model. The Object Model is used by all OMG-compliant technologies such as The Common Object Request Broker: Architecture and Specification (CORBA).

This model defines a common object semantics for specifying the externally visible characteristics of objects in a standard and implementation-independent way. The common semantics characterise objects that exist in an OMG-compliant system.

The externally visible characteristics of objects are described by an interface which consists of operation signatures. The external view of both object behaviour and object state (information needed to alter the outcome of a subsequent operation) are modelled in terms of operation signatures.
The OMG Object Model defines a core set of requirements that must be supported in any system that complies with the Object Model standard. This set of required capabilities is called the Core Object Model and agreement was reached on these capabilities in 1992.

2. Consensus, Fit for Purpose and Availability

OMG's approach to standards is embodied in just a few words - consensus; fit for purpose; availability.

OMG has created a forum where technical specifications can be arrived at through consensus. It has a formal process of issuing RFIs (Requests for Information) and RFPs (Requests for Proposal). These requests are issued by the OMG Technical Committee (TC). The OMG TC supervises Sub Committees, Task Forces and Special Interest Groups (SIGs). Sub Committees include those for Reference Model, and Object Model. Task Forces include those for Object Request Broker (CORBA), CORBAfacilities, and CORBAservices. SIGs include those for End-users, Telecoms, Healthcare, Portable Common Tools Environment (PCTE), Business Object Management, Finance and Security.

A landmark event for OMG and the development of object technology standards was the OMG's adoption of an Object Request Broker (ORB) standard in October 1991. The ORB provides the mechanisms by which objects transparently make and receive requests and responses. In doing so, the ORB provides interoperability between applications on different machines in heterogeneous distributed environments and seamlessly interconnects multiple object systems. A key feature of CORBA is that object interfaces are defined in a standard way using OMG's Interface Definition Language (IDL).

1992 saw the availability of the published CORBA (Common Object Request Broker Architecture) specification and the adoption of CORBA Version 1 by over 50 computer manufacturers and software developers. Public support for CORBA grew during 1993 to embrace over 80 companies. By the end of 1994 over 20 vendor developers were shipping their own CORBA 1 conformant systems.

3. Interoperability - the Only Realistic Goal

OMG believes that a consensus on object (software) interoperability is the only realistic interoperability goal within the domains of software development and software deployment. Objects created in a CORBA 1-based environment can not, necessarily, interoperate with objects created in another CORBA 1-based environment. One of the key elements of the CORBA 2.0 technical specification is that interoperability between any and all CORBA 2.0 created objects is guaranteed.

Agreement of the CORBA 2.0 interoperability specification was reached at the end of 1994. Two final technology submissions were submitted to OMG at the end of September 1994. The Universal Networked Objects (UNO) proposal was made by BNR, Expersoft, IBM, ICL, Iona Technologies and Sun. The DCE Inter-ORB Protocol proposal was made by DEC, Hewlett-Packard and IBM. OMG adopted the UNO proposal in December 1994. The new CORBA 2.0 Interoperability Specification details two-way communication between different vendors' ORB implementations over a mandatory TCP/IP wire protocol and other optional wire transports such as DCE. A General Inter-ORB protocol (GIOP) is a message format hosted on any network transport. TCP/IP is the mandatory transport for CORBA 2.0. CORBA 2.0 also specifies an Environment Specific Inter-ORB Protocol (ESIOP) as an approach for interoperability in DCE. CORBA 1&2 are fully described in an OMG CORBA specification published in August 1995 [2].

At Object World in San Francisco in August 1995, DEC, Expersoft, Fujitsu, Genesis, Hewlett-Packard, Hitachi, IBM, ICL, Iona Technologies, NeXT and Sun all ran live CORBA 2.0-conformant product demonstrations.

Language mapping specifications to OMG CORBA IDL have been agreed for C, C++ and Smalltalk.

In August 1994, Candle, DEC and Microsoft proposed an OLE/COM to CORBA interworking presentation to the OMG TC. The TC voted 38 to 1 to begin the process of drafting an OLE/COM RFP. This two part RFP was issued in April 1995. "Part A" asks for responses for a gateway between existing OLE/COM and CORBA, and "Part B" asks for responses for a gateway for the next major release of OLE/COM with distributed support and CORBA. This RFP drafting was done by representatives from IBM, Microsoft, Sybase and APM. In June 1995, 13 companies submitted Letters of Intent (LOIs) to respond to Part A, with 12 of them also intending to respond to Part B. It is anticipated that the adoption of a specification for technology for OLE/COM to CORBA will occur for "Part A" in late 1995, and for "Part B" in early 1996.

In April 1995, OMG adopted an Interface Repository Specification (jointly submitted by DEC, Hewlett-Packard and SunSoft). This CORBA component specifies low level protocols between ORBs and guarantees interoperability between independently designed ORBs.

A major breakthrough was the definition of the initial set of CORBAservices standards, which was achieved in November, 1993. This standard defines the four common services - Object Naming, Object Events, Life Cycle and Persistent Object Service - on which most of the 16 other OMG identified CORBAservices depend.

In January 1995 OMG adopted Object Transaction, Externalisation, Relationships and Concurrency Control CORBAservices. Nine major on-line transaction processing (OLTP) and OT vendors jointly developed a specification for an Object Transaction Service. The collaborators were Groupe Bull, IBM, ICL, Iona Technologies, Novell, Inc., Sun, Tandem Computers, Tivoli Systems and Transarc Corporation.

The first eight CORBAservices are defined in CORBAservices: Common Object Services Specification Revised Edition March 31, 1995 [3]. By July 1995, a ninth CORBAservice specification had been adopted - Object Query.
The CORBAfacilities Task Force was formed in December 1993. Its mission is to endorse CORBA-conformant OMG IDL code, to enable application interoperability in vertical markets, and to maximise the leverage of existing de facto and de jure standards. The task force issued an RFP for a Compound Document Facility in October 1994. By January 1995 Letters of Intent had been received from IBM, Fujitsu, CI Labs, Apple, Novell and Silicon Graphics. The two technologies being proposed in responses to the RFP are OpenDoc and Fresco. On 30 March 1995 the Task Force issued an RFI on Financial Services and Accounting Facilities.

4. OMG - an Open Process

OMG has constructive close relationships with many standards bodies, industry groups and user groups. These relationships include those with - The American National Standards Institute (ANSI), CFI, The Component Integration Laboratories (CI Labs), CIS, Corporation for Open Systems (COS), COSE, European Computer Manufacturers' Association (ECMA), ESPRIT, EUREKA, Institute of Electrical and Electronic Engineers (IEEE), IMA, International Telecommunication Union-Telecommunications Standardisation (ITU-TS, formerly CCITT), JIPS, National Institute for Standards and Technology (NIST), Network Management Forum (NMF), National Physical Laboratory

(NPL), Object Definition Alliance (ODA), Open Applications Group (OAG), Open Software Foundation (OSF), Open Systems Interconnection/ International Standards Organisation (OSI/ISO), The Petrochemical Open Systems Consortium (POSC), and X-Open.
In early 1994, OMG formed a Special Interest Group (SIG) with the goal of fostering compliance with PCTE and OMG's OMA. This PCTE SIG is also charged with identifying requirements for, and fostering convergence of, interoperable CASE environments and fine grain repository tools for the evolution of PCTE. In addition, the PCTE SIG hopes to work with users, vendors, academia and government, (as well as providing technical liaison staff to work with relevant consortia and accredited standards organisations) to assure consistent requirements for the evolution of PCTE to OMA compliance, object orientation and fine granularity standards.

5. Analysis and Design Methods

There has been a plethora of object analysis and design methods developed and refined over the past four years. OMG believed for many years that there would not be a standard method. OMG made a major contribution to the market place in March 1994, by making available its 'Object Analysis and Design, Description of Methods' report [4] This 200 page report describes, in some detail, 21 different object analysis and design methods in use throughout the world. In July 1994 OMG made available its `Object Analysis and Design, Comparison of Methods' report [5]. This 200 page report compares and contrasts 16 different analysis and design methods.

As most methodologies are in their infancy and still being developed, OMG hopes that these reports will help developers in choosing a methodology.
In May 1995 at the OMG Technical Committee meeting in San Jose there was a re-awakening of interest within OMG and amongst method originators to work together in investigating the feasibility and practicality of method standardisation. OMG in now actively pursuing this work in its Design & Analysis SIG.

CONCLUSION

Object technology is set to bring about a fundamental change to the way we develop, use, re-use, distribute, deploy and maintain computer software.

Object technology generally, and OMG's standards specifically, are likely to have a major impact on software development and the whole of the software industry during the next ten years. Developments in object technology hold out the prospect of the creation of a component-based software industry, in which applications are assembled from components from many sources; which can be

deployed and re-deployed on multiple platforms; and can interoperate with other components and applications in a heterogeneous operating environment.
The role of OMG in creating, by consensus, object technology standards is proving a vital one for the software industry. But the job is nowhere near complete and it will take continued, combined efforts by vendors, users, consultants and educators to bring about the adoption of standards-based object management.

References

1. Soley R M Ph.D. (ed), (1992). *Object Management Architecture Guide, Revision 2.0, September 1.* OMG TC Document 92.11.1. Published by The Object Management Group.

2. OMG (1995). *The Common Object Request Broker: Architecture and Specification, Revision 2.0*, July 1995. Published by The Object Management Group.

3. OMG (1995) CORBAservices : *Common Object Services Specification, Revised Edition*, March 31, 1995, OMG Document Number 95-3-31.

4. Hutt A T F (1994), *Object Analysis and Design, Description of Methods,* © Object Management Group. Published by John Wiley & Sons, Inc. ISBN 0-471-62366-0.

5. Hutt A T F (1994), *Object Analysis and Design, Comparison of Methods,*. © Object Management Group. Published by John Wiley & Sons, Inc. ISBN 0-471-05276-0.

Migrating a Legacy System to Object Technology

by Jack Hassall and Keith Oulton

Abstract

The Open Systems movement of the 1980's and 90's offered users the prospect of hardware platform independent applications running on UNIX. The idea was that with all vendors running a standard UNIX, users could easily move their applications from one vendor's RISC to another. That way they wouldn't be "locked" into a particular vendor's hardware - as they had been on mainframes and minis in the 70's and 80's. Although things haven't worked out quite like that, primarily because each vendor developed its own flavour of UNIX, the move to develop applications on, and migrate applications to UNIX has been a steady one.

The Distributed Applications movement of the 1990's offers users the prospect of software platform independent software. The key enabling technology for this is standardised object technology. The big idea is that you can create an object and be confident that it will interoperate with other objects created by you and other people. For this idea to work, there have to be object standards and wide adoption of these standards.

The initial set of such standards now exists and they have the support of the vast majority of the major computer, software and systems vendors, as well as many of the world's largest end-users.

These standards are the Object Management Group (OMG) CORBA standards. CORBA stands for Common Object Request Broker Architecture and Specification. There are 520 OMG members, which makes it the world's largest software development consortium. During the last six years, OMG has established a whole set of Distributed Applications standards, the most important of which are how objects are defined (OMG Object Model), how objects communicate with each other (OMG CORBA), and how objects are realised and maintained (OMG CORBAservices).

1. CORBA - The Key to Distributed Applications

There are basically three approaches to adopting the OMG standards:

- Implement the CORBA specifications directly, eg as IBM has done in creating its Distributed System Object Model (DSOM).

- Adopt someone else's CORBA implementation, eg Component Integration Laboratories has adopted DSOM to achieve CORBA conformance for its OpenDoc distributed compound document architecture.

- Migrate to CORBA.

This article deals with migrating a legacy application to object technology generally and CORBA specifically.

The project's initiation and execution involved three organisations - IBM UK, Stanford Software and OMG.

In December, 1994 OMG set up its Financial Special Interest Group (F-SIG), the founding chair of which is Jack Hassall, Technical Director of Stockport-based Stanford Software. The F-SIG mission is identifying and recommending for adoption CORBA conformant technical specifications in the financial services sector.

Financial accounting is a common process throughout the world and OMG is working towards creating a standard CORBA-conformant financial accounting standard. The adoption of this standard will enable accounting systems to interoperate with each other and with personal productivity, departmental and enterprise applications.

OMG's F-SIG decided to carry out a design study on migrating an existing legacy accounting system to CORBA. Stanford Software volunteered its Epsilon accounting system as the guinea pig legacy accounting application, and IBM in the UK agreed to work with them on the study. Tom Mowbray, Principal Scientist with the MITRE Corporation, and OMG CORBAfacilities chair was also directly involved in the migration/design study.

2. Legacy Systems

Traditional legacy systems are "vertically integrated" - from the user interface, right down to the very data and devices (see figure 1). Also, legacy systems typically use proprietary formats of one sort or another which in turn, have hardware and software dependencies of their own.

All of these levels of dependency are intermixed in the code, making the system brittle, non-extensible and subject to obsolescence as the underlying hardware and software products evolve. This situation creates many problems, for example, the lack of interoperability between independently developed systems, as well as the lack of portability across different operating systems, hardware platforms and so forth.

It's just a simple a fact of life that the vast majority of end user computing environments are inherently heterogeneous (that is to say, a mix of hardware and software products from different vendors), and put quite simply, traditional legacy systems are poorly suited to integrate and evolve in these environments.

EPSILON.EXE is a classic IBM PC compatible DOS based financial accounting application program, complete with the ubiquitous character based interface and vertically integrated code thrown in for good measure. Epsilon is therefore a suitable subject for a Migration/Design study.

Epsilon was written in the CA-Clipper 5.x language, which is in use by around 2.3 million software developers world-wide. CA-Clipper 5.x features a very limited amount of object-orientation and is modular, open and extensible by design.

Clipper's data manipulation language (DML) has many similarities with other procedurally oriented languages that have been used to implement other legacy software systems. For example, the Clipper development environment supports: #includes, #''defines, locals, statics, arrays, codeblocks, evals, templates, objects, private and public declarations, make files, incremental compilation, incremental linking and so forth, as well as third party software integration using either C, C++ or assembly language.

Epsilon has significant advantages compared to many traditional legacy systems, due to its interoperable data interchange format which is universally known as Xbase. There are approximately 15 million users of Xbase and related technologies world-wide, and Xbase even has its own ANSI Standards Committee (X319J).

3. Exploiting Object Technology

Our intention was to migrate this classic legacy system to Component Software based upon Object Technology. The essence of the migration is the partitioning of the application into reusable components that are integrated through a standards based open architecture framework. Components differ as to their level of re-usability.

On the "bottom" of the architecture are the reusable services and data objects - highly portable back end objects which capture the reusable applications functionality as stable services and data definitions. Other specialised application components are built upon these, adding application specifics such as user interfaces and business processes. Such specialised components can be rapidly developed with advanced visual design tools such as the one used - IBM's VisualAge - and users can achieve "plug and play" capability with reusable software components. Also, these components can be further specialised to meet specific user needs in various and different vertical market areas.

4. Reference Architecture

The Reference Architecture is based upon concepts from Ivar Jacobson, OMG Business Object Management Special Interest Group (BOM-SIG) and other advanced architecture thinkers. The Reference Architecture defines five groups of objects, based on technology source and reusability (see figure 3).

Interface Objects are the user interfaces which can be rapidly generated by products like IBM's VisualAge. Interface Objects are the menus, data entry screens, report generation screens and help screens as well as the text contained in those objects.

Control Objects are organisation specific, providing specialised activation of the reusable objects and interfaces. Control Objects represent software that is specific to an organisation's business processes, such as Workflow. Control Objects are typically accessed by on screen "buttons" and controlling interfaces and provide the functionality and personality to reusable software. Control Objects are the least reusable and most application specific category of objects.

Service Objects represent highly reusable software components that can be used by multiple applications and systems which are back end oriented, portable and platform independent. This group of objects may be thought of as common services or facilities. Service Objects identified in the legacy system include initialisation, report generation, user interface facilities, calendaring, BCD arithmetic and conversion, transaction type management, multi-currency and so forth. Many service objects will be available commercially and can include end-user objects which are unique and high-value for a particular industry.

Data Objects are the persistent objects in the system. These are typically implemented with commercial database technology and provide methods and data (encapsulated as objects). The key is to provide isolation between the storage implementation and the client software in the rest of the system. Data Objects represent the data and its associated processing and provide encapsulated access through object-oriented message interfaces as well as providing isolation between the

Client software and the data implementation/representation.

Technology Objects are the enabling standards and commercial products that enable the implementations of the system using Object Technology.

5. Escaping the Tyranny of Hierarchical Menus and Procedural Constraints

Like many legacy systems, the actual business functionality that is delivered to the user is driven by a series of hierarchical menus. These menus serve as nothing more than a simple launchpad for the executable functions that comprise the legacy system, yet represent a very large percentage of the legacy code.

One of the drawbacks of this is clearly illustrated by examining the behaviour of the systems Purchase Order Entry executable function, which is invoked when the user wants to buy in goods and/or services for their organisation. The user cannot enter a new Purchase Order for an item unless that item has already been entered into a table which stores the organisation's inventory on disk.

This makes good business sense, because the user of the software can't randomly buy something that isn't traceable. However, by using conventional, procedural technology to implement the software in the first place, the enforcement of this business rule in the software can cause things to get unnecessarily complicated.

Suppose our end user wants to buy some paper clips for their organisation. The user selects the Purchase Order Menu from the Main System Menu and presses the [Enter] key over the appropriate executable function. They select a source supplier from the supplier table, enter the date and so forth.

The business rule then informs the user that "Paper Clips" have not been entered into the stock table and the hierarchical menu scheme forces the user to "back out" to the Purchase Ledger menu.

The user is then forced to select the Stock Control menu from the Main System menu and invoke the executable function which allows them to enter "Paper Clips" into the stock table. After you've done all this, you can then go back and raise the purchase order for your paper clips.

Of course for very long time, a large number of the systems business users only ever purchased items that were "in stock", so this problem only became visible (with the value of hindsight), when somebody else pointed it out whose business involved the purchase of many new stock items "on the fly".

This is yet another classic example of the inevitable need to adapt the behaviour of software systems generally, which is always due to some unexpected requirement that could never have been foreseen.

6. Uncoupling Vertically Integrated Code

Vertically integrated code makes this a tricky problem to solve without writing even more vertically integrated code, however, this is a good, common-sense business rule that needs to be preserved.

For example, as a software developer, you would have to locate and re-code the Purchase Order Entry executable function in order to make it check whether or not the stock item was physically recorded in the stock table. If it wasn't, you'd have to do something.

For example, you'd have to bring up a screen allowing the user to describe and save the new stock item "on the fly", which involves more coding and further distribution headaches. Or, you'd have to make some modification or other to the original program to solve this unexpected side-effect, that resulted from the enforcement of a business rule which not only seemed to make sense at design time, it still does. To change this situation or mode of operation in the legacy system, you simply have to write some code.

It's also worth mentioning that you would have to multiply the apparent measure of complexity by the number of platforms that you intend to support (as a bare minimum), in order to even begin thinking about the actual level of complexity involved with the planning, implementation and delivery of such a modification, and all of this on the grounds that you are just trying to solve an apparently simple yet frustrating problem such as this one in this example.

After a rigorous analysis of the legacy system, as well as the migration and physical implementation of key parts, it is now both clear (and demonstrable) that the aforementioned problem can be completely eliminated without writing a single line of code.

The newly migrated menu system allows the user to switch directly from the Purchase Order Entry executable function to the Stock Control Menu with just one mouse click and subsequently activate the "Adjust Stock In" executable function with a double click, should the aforementioned situation arise.

After entering and saving the new stock item into the stock table, the user reselects the Purchase Order Entry executable function with a single mouse click and continues. The main point to be made here is that an unanticipated functional deficiency was completely eliminated during the migration process and that the original business rule was preserved without any performing coding whatsoever.

The new prototype menu system is a totally object oriented and legacy system compatible front end, which is graphical, fully extensible and offers many exciting distribution and organisational capabilities that just weren't possible with the original legacy system. The migration of the entire legacy menu system was made possible by inheriting from just two readily available base classes and was migrated, delivered and fully operational within two weeks.

7. Common Functionality

One very singular type of behaviour in the legacy system was identified and a test implementation commenced immediately to see if we could rapidly migrate a single data entry/maintenance type of executable function from the existing legacy system to Object Technology and CORBA in record time.

Common functionality available throughout the system was identified in a single, stereotypical executable function that when invoked:

saved the current runtime environment initialised the environment to suit itself; opened the customer table in the Epsilon database; executed a query on the first row of the table; displayed the results of the query on the screen; and waited for one of several possible commands from the user

The overall behaviour exhibited by the executable function under consideration, represents an extremely high percentage of the overall legacy system's data entry, browsing and maintenance capabilities, and if this common functionality could be encapsulated into an abstract object class, it would then be possible to inherit and subclass this base functionality and rapidly populate around 50% of the new system with subtly different specialisations of this class, which comprises much of the original legacy system.

Basic business data, such as customer information, is entered into the system an entity at a time, which can subsequently be scrolled, backwards and forwards as well as edited, queried on (searched for a specific entity), deleted (only if in accordance with embedded business rules), as well as an option to select the logical order in which the entities are displayed and a "gateway" to other executable functions, that operate directly on the selected entity, as well as an exit button to close the executable function.

8. The Tools for the Job

To implement the prototype, we used IBM's VisualAge Team product, which is an object-oriented visual application development environment, that allows applications to be assembled using pre-fabricated components which represent the Client/Server spectrum. In other words, a RAD tool.

Applications are built by drawing "connections" between these pre-fabricated parts (objects) on the VDU. The version of VisualAge that we used during this part of the study was for the Smalltalk language, running under the OS/2 Warp operating system.

The resultant executable function as it stands runs under a number of different platforms, such as OS/2 Warp, MS-Windows xx and AIX as well as on RS/6000 platforms. IBM's Smalltalk implementation also supports an easy and gradual way to subsequently migrate SOM and DSOM (IBM's CORBA implementation), once we have made the initial transition from procedural technology to Object Technology.

A working prototype of a key executable function from the legacy system was migrated and delivered in less than a week and the table structure and indexes from the existing legacy system were migrated to IBM's DB2/2 database at the same time.

Building a small, reusable and key executable function, has allowed us to experiment, refine and greatly simplify the requirements for obtaining the desired functionality from the class, which in the original legacy executable function comprised over 800 lines of source code. Existing data from the legacy system was imported into DB2/2 intact, allowing us to see the new code in action and assess the performance of the prototype system. This approach is always much easier than guessing what something is going to be like because you haven't got large quantities of control data.

Once this basic class has been perfected, the results can be "fed back" to the abstract base class, which can then be inherited from and subclassed into the various "specialisations", which will result in the migration of approximately 50% of the legacy applications' executable functionality, with instances of a known and stable object.

At the time of writing (August 95), there's still quite a way to go, and although our initial abstract Epsilon Controller Class isn't quite perfect, it soon will be, and we hope that as a direct result of this migration study, we have been able to share some important ideas with the reader regarding the migration of legacy systems in general to Object Technology and CORBA.

9. Conclusions

The migration of legacy systems to Object Technology and CORBA is not only feasible but can also yield substantial benefits for all sizes of projects and organisations, from entry-level PC software to Volume End Users with mainframe software systems.

However, the naive application of Object Technology does not yield substantial benefits. There is an acute need to focus on system architecture and design for reusability, abstraction and product and subsystem isolation as well as many other principles, in order to exploit the true benefits of Object Technology, which are substantial, such as rapid application development and system extensibility.

Biographies and Contact Information:

Keith Oulton is a Consultant with IBM UK Ltd having 11 years experience in Information Technology, working with client IT, Business Executives and End users. His experience began in programming 3GL applications, rapidly moving to Client/Server technology 7 years ago. Keith has provided Client/Server consultancy, mainly in the Financial Services sector and is now applying that knowledge to support and grow the business opportunities in the marketplace today using Object Technology.

Keith Oulton
Consultant
IBM UK Ltd
Jackson House
Sibson Road
Sale
Cheshire
WA14 4UD
Tel: 0161 905 6664
Fax: 0161 969 6108
email: Keith_Oulton@UK.IBM.COM

Jack Hassall is the Technical Director of Standford Software and has been involved in IT since 1982. Jack is a contributing author to the OMG's Common Facilities Architecture and is the Chairman of the OMG's Financial Services Special Interest Group (OMG F-SIG).

Jack Hassall
Technical Director
Stanford Software
The Hollygate
Chestergate
Stockport
Cheshire
SK3 0BD
Tel: 0161 480 4051/7064
Fax: 0161 429 0966
email: 100277,2260

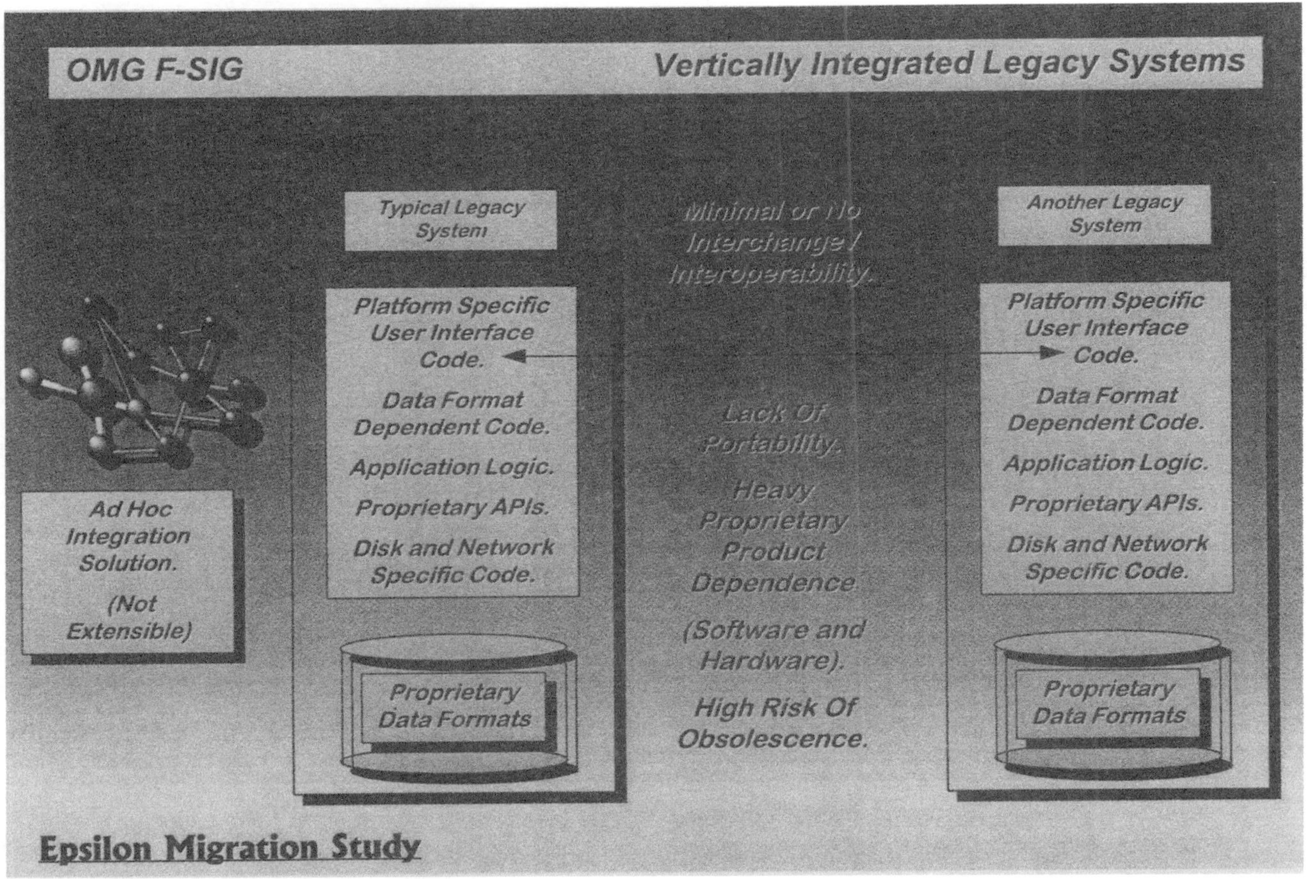

OMG F-SIG
Vertically Integrated Legacy Systems
Typical Legacy System
Minimal or No Interchange / Interoperability.
Another Legacy System
Platform Specific User Interface Code.
Data Format Dependent Code.
Application Logic.
Proprietary APIs.
Disk and Network Specific Code.
Lack Of Portability.
Heavy Proprietary Product Dependence
(Software and Hardware).
High Risk Of Obsolescence.
Platform Specific User Interface Code.
Data Format Dependent Code.
Application Logic.
Proprietary APIs.
Disk and Network Specific Code.
Ad Hoc Integration Solution.
(Not Extensible)
Proprietary Data Formats
Proprietary Data Formats
Epsilon Migration Study

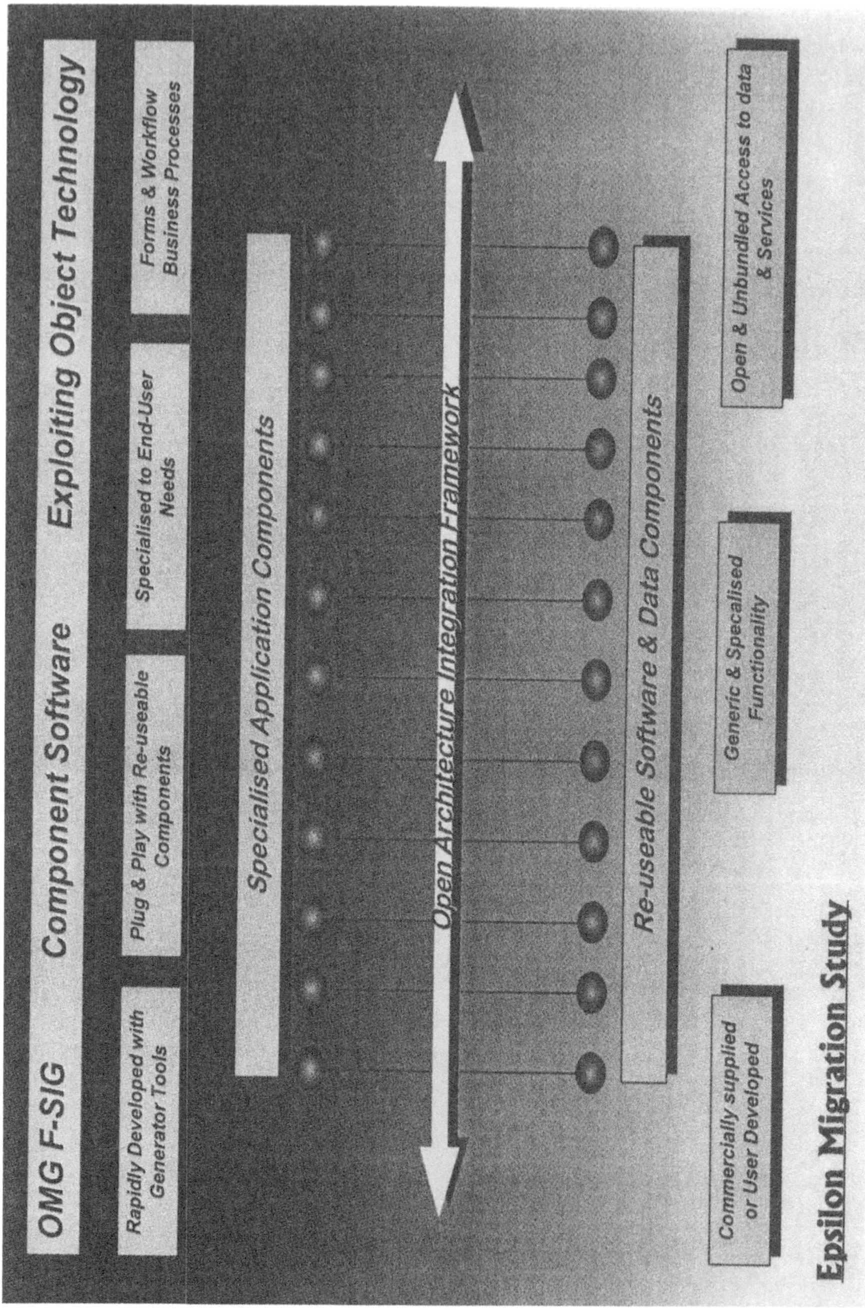
OMG F-SIG
Component Software
Exploiting Object Technology
Rapidly Developed with Generator Tools
Plug & Play with Re-useable Components
Specialised to End-User Needs
Forms & Workflow Business Processes
Specialised Application Components
Open Architecture Integration Framework
Re-useable Software & Data Components
Commercially supplied or User Developed
Generic & Specialised Functionality
Open & Unbundled Access to data & Services
Epsilon Migration Study

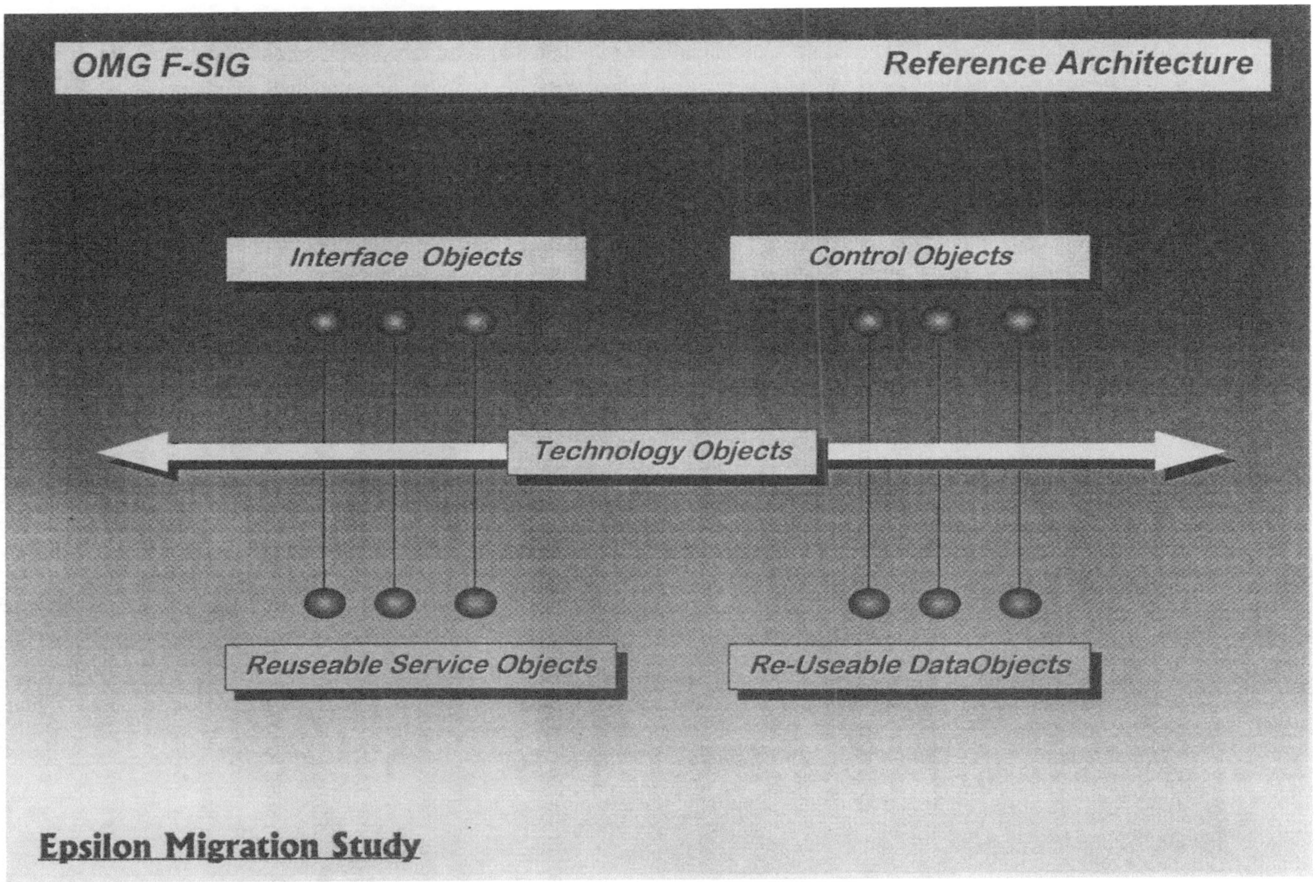
OMG F-SIG
Reference Architecture
Interface Objects
Control Objects
Technology Objects
Reuseable Service Objects
Re-Useable DataObjects
Epsilon Migration Study

A Pragmatic Approach to Reuse Introduction in an Industrial Setting

Ben Whittle, Wing Lam and Tim Kelly
Rolls-Royce University Technology Centre
University of York, York, YO1 5DD, UK
[ben,wing,tpk]@minster.york.ac.uk

Abstract

The Rolls-Royce University Technology Centre at the University of York has spent the past two years introducing a reuse initiative in the Control Systems Engineering department of Rolls-Royce Aerospace in Derby, England. During this time reuse has begun the progression from an 'ad hoc' adjunct to the system production process to a systematic, well managed and organised core technique. This paper will explain the key features and pragmatics of reuse introduction.

Keywords: reuse, introduction, industrial, aerospace.

1. Introduction

In order to understand reuse introduction we must know what we are trying to achieve. We use the following definition of reuse:

Reuse is the planned use of systems artifacts and processes in the development of solutions to similar problems.

The important features of this definition are that reuse is:

- planned: there is a defined means of achieving a known level of reuse.
- system artifacts and processes: we are considering more than the reuse of code. A greater advantage (often termed reuse leverage) can be gained by reuse of related artifacts (requirements, design, code, tests etc.) from different stages of the lifecycle. Process is important for reuse. The process must be defined in such a way that it embodies reuse principles (e.g. ensuring that the engineer has available and selects appropriate reusable components) but we can also reuse the process. If the same process is used, we are more likely to achieve reuse as similar artifacts are likely to be created.
- similar problems: if reuse is to be successful then there must be some common factor in the problem that enables us to define a reusable artifact. For example, the common factor could be an algorithm, an architectural style or a data set. What we must be able to do is to find suitable analogies and abstractions, ways

of separating the part of the problem which doesn't change from that which does, e.g. separating an algorithm from the data it operates on.

We believe that in the magority of organisations reuse is simply good engineering practice. For example, reuse includes planning for the products as a series or family and defining a common core of artifacts and a suitable process from which to build them. The kind of reuse where you define a set of parts to build new systems is termed generational. The new system is built from a kit of parts and a style of integration.

Reuse can also be compositional, taking small existing parts to build the new system. We would also contend that reuse is not new, but is just a name for something the organisation already does. Rarely are new products built completely from scratch, one can't forget years of training and experience, this knowledge exists in the engineering and corporate memory. One approach to reuse is to use case based reasoning techniques [1] to capture experience which can then be used to solve similar problems. Reuse is a natural problem solving techniques. Engineers will commonly have a directory of small chunks of 'useful' code that they cut and paste in solving a new problem, this is often termed 'ad hoc' reuse (although cut and paste is easier to remember). Achieving reuse isn't about forgetting the idea of 'cut and paste', but to understand the benefits that reuse can give us and be able to achieve those benefits through a greater degree of rigour. Systematic reuse [2] must be:

- planned
- managed
- organised
- supported

These are the topics that are covered in this paper.

Before you begin a reuse program you must consider what your organisation is trying to achieve. There must be an organisational goal towards which a reuse program will contribute. One way to think of this is that 'reuse is a means - not an end'. For example, in the case of Rolls-Royce Aerospace [3, 4] the company wanted to achieve a reduction in the costs and timescales of systems production, the reduction was the goal, reuse was one contributing technique. Framing reuse adoption in terms of an organisational goal, particularly one with a stated benefit e.g. a 10% cost reduction, gives you a target to base your estimates on and to examine the long term cost/benefit of the reuse program.

Two frequent questions from managers and engineers will be: 'how much effort should we put into reuse? how much benefit should we expect?'. Once the organisation has considered the goal that reuse will contribute towards and the benefit that can be expected (these steps are considered in Section 2) a judgment can be made on the appropriate level of resource for the reuse effort in relation to the expected benefit. Knowing the goal against which you are measured also provides an easy yardstick against which to measure reuse success. For example, if the goal is to reduce costs then reuse benefits should be measured in terms of cost.

The second section of the paper describes a process for reuse introduction based on the ideas presented in the introduction. Section 3 considers the constraints that reuse places on funding, organisation and strategy. Section 4 draws together the lessons from the paper and Section 5 provides a short conclusion.

2. Introducing Reuse

Section 1 established the background for reuse introduction, defining reuse and stating that reuse introduction should be seen as a means of achieving an organisational goal. This section looks at the reuse introduction process in more detail, providing an outline of the key stages in the process, and following this with a more detailed consideration of each phase. The process we describe in this section is based on that described in [5] which we have modified in the light of our experiences and consideration of domain, culture and organisation.

Any explanation of a process must tread a fine line between generalisation and the provision explanation and examples which target one particular organisation or domain. The remainder of this section treads this line, with references provided at the end of the paper to give more detail on reuse adoption in different domains.

2.1 Steps In Reuse Introduction

The following list outlines the main phases needed in reuse introduction. These phases are intended to be largely sequential. Some phases, such as program definition and the development of reuse strategies, may occur in parallel.

- **initiate program** - decide that reuse is a likely option to help in achieving one or more organisational goals and obtain resources to proceed.
- **define program** - define the scope of the reuse introduction, particularly the domain you wish to improve and the improvements you would like reuse to contribute towards.
- **develop reuse strategies** - select and develop appropriate strategies, and show how the strategies can be linked together, i.e. an incremental approach.
- **analyse strategies and select** - enable the selection of the most appropriate strategy.
- **develop action plan** - develop an implementation plan for the chosen strategy.
- **implement** - put the plan into action.
- **monitor and improve** - measure the plan against the action plan and the organisational goals it is intended to contribute to.

The remainder of Section 2 describes each of the phases in more detail, describing the main steps, key roles, outputs and results expected from each phase. An example, from the authors' experience of reuse introduction is given to illustrate the phase.

2.2 Initiate Program

Main steps:

- identify opportunity for reuse - one way to do this is to try and look for areas of commonality in the products. For example, there may be common services provided, the products may have a common architectural base such as a client server approach, or may all require access to a particular database package.
- identify relevant organisation objectives - there are a great many ways that reuse can contribute to the organisation. Many of the likely contributions are grouped around a reduction in development costs and the related issues of timescales, productivity and quality. However there are other areas where reuse can provide a benefit such as reducing maintenance and migration problems through more appropriate product design.
- Perform and initial cost benefit analysis.

Key roles:

- reuse zealot - there should be someone in the organisation who is keen and confident enough about reuse to push this phase through.

Outputs:

- a short memo detailing the opportunity for reuse and asking for support for further investigation. This memo should contain the initial cost benefit analysis.

Results:

- obtain the commitment for the following stages to define the program and develop the strategies from a resource manager.

Example:
Rolls-Royce had already identified the need to reduce costs and timescales as part of their internal process improvement initiatives. Rolls-Royce management had recognised that engine control systems are developed for a series of engines and therefore the engine controller could enhance the series or family based approach. The Rolls-Royce University Technology Centre (UTC), at the University of York, was asked to help with reuse introduction and provided reuse expertise. Ben Whittle began the workpackage by familiarising himself with the basics of the aero-engine domain and the organisation. Access to middle management and key design engineers enabled the collection of key information which was used in the production of an initial report.

2.3 Define Program

The program definition and development of reuse strategy stages are linked and provide the information on which to base the commitment to proceed with reuse adoption. We have separated them in this description to highlight the difference in the level of abstraction. The definition of the program is concerned with the business as a whole, and although it focuses on reuse it could be part of a larger process improvement initiative.

Main steps:

- define adoption objectives, restate the reasons for considering reuse introduction and quantify them in terms of the benefit that this would yield to the organisation.
- assess the potential for improvement with regard to the objectives, this stage is often part of a process referred to as domain analysis. Domain analysis is a similar process to requirements analysis, but in which the analyst considers the business opportunities at the level of a family of systems or products or a market sector rather than as individual systems. A domain analysis includes a consideration of current capability and market i.e. the business area. A domain analysis should use techniques that the organisation is familiar with so that the analysis can be carried out without having to learn and adopt new techniques and so that the results can easily be interpreted throughout the organisation.

Key roles:
The production of the domain analysis and reuse adoption objectives will require business and systems analysis skills.

Outputs:
A short report detailing the quantified objectives and benefits, and the key results of the domain analysis.

Results:
Establishment of quantified reuse adoption goals and areas of opportunity within the domain for consideration in the development of reuse strategies.

Example:
Work on the program definition and strategy occurred simultaneously in the Rolls-Royce Systems and Software University Technology Centre (UTC) reuse workpackage. The fine grain problem associated with the development of the reuse strategies provided a great deal of input, and convincing technical detail, for the higher level analysis of program definition.
The organisational objectives identified by Rolls-Royce were a quantifiable and measured contribution towards a reduction in costs and timescales of production, whilst retaining (at least) the same quality of production. One particular engine series was defined as the most likely target for the impact of the technology and the development of suitable strategies. The opportunities for reuse and impediments to reuse were framed in terms of the timescales of this project.

2.4 Develop Reuse Strategies

Main steps:

- identify constraints/opportunities for reuse, constraints could include the current organisational structure, team skills, technology and tools availability, for example. Opportunities might include technologies where the company has a market lead or a family of products that will have many similar characteristics.
- identify possible strategies, there will be many ways of achieving reuse from relatively straightforward libraries of components to more sophisticated application generator tools. It will be important to provide a prototype solution of the likely strategies to improve the reusers' (line engineers') confidence in the strategy and possibly provide a strategic advantage to a current product. For example, if the strategy development team can put in the effort to show that the strategy can work for a small area of one product on the line they will win the support and backing of a line manager and possibly several (previously skeptical) engineers.
- cost/benefit analysis of strategies, providing a prototype also enable you to firm up some of the costs for implementing the reuse strategy, giving more credibility to the cost/benefit.

Key roles:
At this stage you need someone who knows the finer points of reuse, a reuse guru, together with an experienced product engineer with an enlightened view of both the product and the process.

Output:
A report detailing the constraints opportunities and strategies including a cost benefit analysis against the costs described in the previous phase.

Result:
A definition of likely strategies, a prototype implementation of some of the strategies and buy in from some of the line engineers and mangers.

Example:
The constraints on the Rolls-Royce reuse were that we knew that the design of some parts of the system would change, although there was still uncertainty as to the final impact of these changes in customer requirements on the design. There were also more precise technical constraints such as the size of the object code and the use of particular source code languages for safety critical systems. The Rolls-Royce strategies were based on the production of a generic extensible architecture providing flexibility to respond to change. The strategies also included a strong element of leverage through the lifecycle e.g. we would use reuse of the system specification to force reuse of the design, the code and the test specifications.

2.5 Analyse Strategies And Select

Main steps:
This stage will probably be carried out in a meeting with a senior manager. Having support (with figures to back it up) from the area in which you have developed the prototype will be useful. It may be useful to provide an input for the following three points to help the manager to select a strategy.

- asses risks of strategies
- analyse organisational readiness for change
- analyse economics of strategies

Key roles:

- Members of the teams who have completed the program definition and strategy analysis stages.
- A suitable manager or team of managers to decide on resource allocation.

Output:
A documented decision on which strategy or strategies to adopt. It may be possible to persuade the manager to adopt one low risk strategy and provide funds for the investigation of a more radical longer term solution.

Result:
A decision, resource allocation and commitment to proceed with a full reuse introduction.

Example:
Rolls-Royce decided to fund an R&D initiative to investigate more advanced techniques including domain specific architecture and application generator technology. As well as implementing a baseline of reuse introduction (a library of requirements, design and code components) on a current project based on the strategy prototyping work.

2.6 Develop Action Plan

Main steps:
The contents of the action plan will differ depending on the characteristics of the organisation, but are likely to include:

- tasks and staffing, the major tasks and resource needs. Remember that just because there is a library there may not necessarily be a full complement of components. It may be better to develop a small number of components and properly configure them rather than expending initial effort on a library. Projects may be encouraged to develop or re-engineer some of the components for submission to the library. Be careful to separate out one-off costs of reuse introduction, such as development or acquisition of tools, from recurring costs such as helping projects to use the library, and component development and maintenance.

- equipment tools and facilities, the library team will need a certain amount of tools, and office space. There are an increasing number of reuse products on the market and it may well be possible to buy a library system, for example, rather than creating your own.
- success criteria and data collection targets, success criteria should be linked to the organisational objectives that reuse has been set up to contribute to. For example, if you contend that reuse will reduce costs and timescales then at a macro level measurement of the success of reuse adoption should be made in terms of costs and timescales. However at the micro level you may wish to look at the way that reuse is being implemented. At the micro level measures such as which library components are being used, how much does it cost to create a new library component, and how long before the investment in a new component pays off will be useful.
- schedule and resource profile, the profile should highlight the development time before a complete reuse system is in place, and the potential impact on future projects.

Key roles:
Reuse project manager to define the plan.
Line managers to review the costs, timescales and impact of the plan.

Output:
A reviewed reuse action plan.

Result:
A commitment to the implementation of the plan.

Example:
Two separate introduction plans were produced, one for the more advanced R&D project and another for reuse introduction on the current project. The plans also showed where the more advanced technology could be brought into the line developments, once it had been proven, and how this would influence future projects.

2.7 Implement, Monitor And Improve

Main steps:
The implementation will consist of two phases a 'reuse start up' when the technology and process changes, and the subsequent development using the reuse tools and techniques. The previous section indicated the two levels of monitoring that are likely to be necessary to ensure that reuse is properly introduced and that it contributes to the organisations' objectives. Once reuse has been introduced it should be possible to regard it as another facet of the normal engineering process and use the standard process improvement mechanism to influence reuse uptake.

Key roles:
Reuse champion - to ensure that the reuse effort does lose direction or impetus.

Reuse manager - this could be a combined technical and managerial role, it involves ensuring that the day to day issue of component generation and usage are carried out. The managerial role could be combined with the role of reuse design leader or chief librarian (not a very inspiring title). A key engineer who assist new projects in the design and development of and with reusable components.

Output:
A reuse program which has a positive impact on the organisations projects.

Result:
Progress towards the organisations stated objectives.

Example:
The reuse adoption work at Rolls-Royce is well underway. The first engine controller in the series is almost completed and the second is in production. There is a high level of reuse between them at the current time, a measurement of the affects of reuse on costs and timescales is underway.

3. Strategy, Funding and Organisation

Section 2 described a reuse introduction process highlighting the technical and managerial aspects of reuse introduction. This section briefly examines some of the other aspects of reuse adoption, funding and organisation, and the development of a reuse strategy. For further examples of reuse introduction in specific organisations or domains see [6, 7] respectively.

3.1 Strategy

A reuse strategy is a good way of describing both what you think reuse should achieve and ways in which reuse could be achieved. The reuse strategy is the basis for reuse implementation. Once reuse adoption is under way the strategy forms a reference for engineers within the team and should be regularly revisited and updated. The list below illustrates a typical contents sheet for a reuse strategy document with brief examples from Rolls-Royce Aerospace:

- Aims and Goals - to contribute to a reduction in costs and timescales of X% per year over the next 5 years.
- Description of approach - a generic and extensible domain specific architecture.
- Cost benefit analysis
- Example scenario - a description of how reuse will be achieved in the starting subsystem for the engine controller on the current project.

Each department and lifecycle phase should be encouraged to develop their own reuse strategy document and show how it contributes to the whole. For example, the testing group strategy says that the group will endeavour to reuse test scripts where reuse of requirements, design and code enable this, and in addition will develop generic test templates for particular regularly occurring tests.

3.2 Funding

Funding and organisational issues strike to the very core of the company. It is likely that the company would like to relate funding of reuse to usage of the reused components [8, 9 and 10]. This places a heavy burden on the library, to record the usage of components and to place a value on the benefit of using a component (which may or may not be related to its production cost). There are two key phases to consider:

- initiation - building up the components and the tools - who pays to set up the reuse structure. For example, it would seem that none of the company's projects are likely to benefit during the reuse initiation phase. It would seem that projects that do not benefit are unlikely to want to pay for reuse, particularly if the projects are in the mature stages. We suggest that reuse initiation should be centrally funded as part of a general process improvement budget.
- operation - developing and maintaining components - charging for usage. One option is to continue to pay for reuse from central resources. However this would seem to be unfair to projects which, for some perfectly good reason, will not make use of all the library resources. A compromise must be made between the cost of measurement and the utility of charging for component use.

3.3 Organisation

The issue of organisation is related to funding. Should there be a separate team developing components or should reuse occur with the existing project teams? A number of common models [11] have been identified of which the following are particularly interesting:

- nested producer - the producer of the reusable component is a member of a project team but produces components that are given to the library or marketed to other project teams.
- producer pool - two or more projects set up a common team to work on shared problems.
- producer team - a separate team is set up to develop and administer the reuse effort.

The choice of organisational model depends very much on the characteristics of the company and the flexibility of the company's organisational structure. However most organisations that have reported a great deal of successful reuse consider the producer team to be the most appropriate organisation structure. The main reasons for the choice of the team producer model appears to be that the team is not under the direction or management of any particular project.

4. Lessons

The following key lessons about reuse introduction have been distilled over the past two years, see [3, 4 and 12]:

- be realistic
- show short term payback - i.e. an incremental approach is good
- the generation of a fancy library won't give you good components - invest in the components and provide an initial configuration structure that can be expanded
- define a strategy that brings the company/department to a baseline, doing basic reuse so that you influence the culture before trying the latest reuse techniques
- cultural problems dominate the technical problems - get the engineers on your side
- case study/demo is a good way of getting people on your side and developing links with those who will have to implement the reuse program. The results of the study provide you with additional information for cost benefit analyses.

5. Conclusions

This paper has focused on the reuse introduction process as a means of transferring and tailoring technologies without covering any of the technologies in particular. Beware of those who would 'sell' you 'one size fits all' techniques, which may or may not be appropriate for your organisation. In the majority of cases a large change in technology is inappropriate as it will cost you a great deal in terms of training and tools and will not increase reuse in the short to medium term. Changing to an Object Oriented method, for example, should be seen as a separate process improvement activity, that will have an influence, possibly negative in the short term, on reuse, but is neither necessary or sufficient to achieve reuse. Reuse is a conservative technology that resists the impact of change.

This paper has placed a heavy emphasis on planning, organisation and management of reuse adoption. Most companies will be new to reuse and will not know what to expect. There will be no initial empirical foundation for the reuse estimates. The technology and ideas must evolve from the reuse strategies. The process will be iterative with the strategies being redefined as a result of reuse adoption experience. The generation of appropriate empirical data will enable better future estimates of the impact of reuse on project timescales and provide a focus for improvements.

6. Acknowledgements

The authors acknowledge the financial support given by Rolls-Royce plc. for the work reported in this paper. The authors would also like to acknowledge the

assistance of staff in Rolls-Royce Aerospace, RoSEC and the Rolls-Royce University Technology Centre at the University of York.
Rolls-Royce: C Jack, J Kelly, E Williams, P Summers, A Mowles.
RoSEC: J Hill, R Rimmer, K Harper.
York UTC: J McDermid, T Jackson, I Bate, A Vickers, P Tongue.

7. References and Further Reading

[1] 'Guest Editors Introduction', IEEE Expert, 7(5) pages 5-6, 1992.

[2] William Frakes and Sadahiro Isoda, Guest Editors, `Systematic Reuse', special issue of IEEE Software, 11(5) September 1994.

[3] J Hill, K Harper, J McDermid, R Rimmer, B Whittle, 'The Development of Reusable Engine Control Technology for Application in Future Engines', Royal Aeronautical Society Conference Bristol 3rd and 4th of November 1994.

[4] J Hill, K Harper, J McDermid, R Rimmer, B Whittle, M Yates, 'Reuse of Engine Control Technology', 1994 Avionics Conference and Exhibition 'Systems Integration is the Sky the Limit?' Heathrow 30th November - 1st December.

[5] Software Productivity Consortium, 'Reuse Adoption Guidebook' version 01.00.03 SPC-92051-CMC (November 1992).

[6] Rebecca Joos, 'Software Reuse at Motorola', in [1], pages 42-47.

[7] James O'Connor, Catharine Mansour, Jerri Turner-Harris and Grady Campbell, 'Reuse in Command and Control Systems', in [1], pages 70-79.

[8] Wayne Lim, 'Effects of Reuse on Quality Productivity and Economics', in [1], pages 23-30.

[9] T Frazier, E Bailey, and B Angier, 'Economic Foundations for Pricing Software Reuse Repositories', Institute for Defense Analyses Paper P-2975, prepared for the Office of the Assistant Secretary of Defense, IDA 1801 N. Beauregard Street, Alexandria, Virginia, September 1994.

[10] J Poulin, 'Populating Software Repositories: Incentives and Domain-Specific Software', accepted for publication in Journal of Systems and Software, September 1995.

[11] Danielle Fafchamps, 'Organisational Factors and Reuse', in [1], pages 31-41.

[12] T Kelly, W Lam & B Whittle, `A Flexible Approach to Constructing Virtual Reuse Libraries', Workshop on Software Reuse, Morganstown, West Virginia, USA, August 1995.

Author Index

GPSR Compliance

The European Union's (EU) General Product Safety Regulation (GPSR) is a set of rules that requires consumer products to be safe and our obligations to ensure this.

If you have any concerns about our products, you can contact us on ProductSafety@springernature.com

In case Publisher is established outside the EU, the EU authorized representative is:

Springer Nature Customer Service Center GmbH
Europaplatz 3
69115 Heidelberg, Germany

Batch number: 10583998

Printed by Printforce, the Netherlands